100 Great Recipes

Baking

100 Great Recipes

Baking

Ann Nicol

**BARNES
& NOBLE**

NEW YORK

This edition published by Barnes & Noble Publishing, Inc.,
By arrangement with D&S Books Ltd

2006 Barnes & Noble Books

M 10 9 8 7 6 5 4 3 2 1

ISBN 0-7607-8099-4

Creative Director: Sarah King
Editor: Debbie Key
Project Editor: Nicola Barber
Photographer: Paul Forrester/Colin Bowling
Designer: Debbie Fisher

© 2005 D&S Books Ltd

Printed in China

Contents

Introduction

Introduction

There's something extremely satisfying about real home baking and the sense of achievement you get when you have made a fresh batch of cakes for your family. The comforting aroma of baking that fills the house, and the mouth-watering moment when you first bite into a golden, crumbly cake, are well worth the effort.

We all lead busy lives these days, and most people say they don't have time for home baking. The tradition of baking may end up becoming more of a hobby. But if you want to take time out from the stresses of modern life, why not indulge in the therapeutic delights of baking? There is no better way of relaxing than kneading a dough, or beating a fluffy, buttery mixture. If you are worried about giving your family manufactured foods containing chemical additives, colorings, preservatives, and excess salt, you will find home baking solves this problem. You'll have total control over the ingredients you use in baking, and, don't forget, there is a good range of organic and additive-free ingredients and organic eggs now available in supermarkets.

100 Great Recipes—Baking provides a delicious range of recipes for cakes, cookies, and teabreads, and you'll find sweet and savory pastry dishes as well (ideal for packing into lunch boxes). You can be creative with yeasted breads and bakes, or make traditional favorites. Whole-wheat flours need special treatment, so there is a separate section on these, including some vegetarian recipes, too. Also included are larger cakes baked in baking trays for cutting into squares. You will find this section useful if you are ever asked to bake for a bake sale or school gala. For formal occasions, there are some mouth-watering gateaux requiring a little more preparation. Chocolate must be the most popular ingredient in baking, so I've included plenty of recipes using dark, white, and milk chocolate, cocoa powder, grated, melted, and chocolate chips. I have also added a recipe made from carob for those who are allergic to chocolate.

This book is aimed at those who are new to baking and also experienced bakers. In *100 Great Recipes—Baking*, I have chosen step-by-step recipes with pictures, showing you how to create lovely bakes in easy stages. There are cakes for every occasion, some very quick and easy, some requiring a little more time. You'll find cakes for special occasions, such as birthdays, or simple, plain cookies and teabreads that go well with a cup of tea. So, choose your favorite recipe and start baking now. Fill the kitchen with the aroma of freshly baked cakes and sit back and wait for the comments of admiration.

Tips for Success

Here are some baking tips that will help you to achieve the best results, so follow these for success.

Oven Temperatures

I usually begin each recipe with the oven temperature. It does make a difference if you preheat the oven to the correct temperature before placing the cake in to bake.

- Always preheat the oven in plenty of time, and arrange the shelves in the correct position in the oven.

- If you have a convection oven, these circulate hot air around the oven and heat up very quickly. For these ovens, you will need to reduce the temperature by 10% and you may also need to reduce the cooking time as well. Follow your manufacturer's instruction leaflet and get to know the way your oven heats up for success.

- **TOO HOT** Remember, if the oven is too hot, the outside of a cake will burn before the inside has had time to cook.

- **TOO COOL** Remember, if the oven is too cool, this may cause cakes to sink or rise unevenly.

- Don't open the oven door until at least halfway through the baking time, or the rising process will be interrupted. This will cause a sudden drop in temperature that will stop the cake expanding and make it sink.

Pans

- Always use the size of pan stated in the recipe, or else your cakes will turn out too shallow, will peak, crack, or even sink in the middle.

- Choose good-quality, rigid, nonstick bakeware. If you are buying new pans, it is a good investment to pay a little more. Good-quality pans will last much longer and give better results. Cheaper bakeware, particularly baking sheets, may bend and buckle during baking.

Preparing Pans

Each recipe gives instructions on how to prepare and line the pans. These are important stages, so don't be tempted to skimp on these as the time and expense in making a cake may be wasted if you cannot turn the cake out of the pan.

- Pans without a nonstick finish need to be greased and lined before use.

- Nonstick pans need only a light greasing, but it is still advisable to line the bases of pans to ensure that the cake can be released easily.

- Apply a thin film of melted vegetable margarine to pans with a pastry brush, or rub around the pan with a paper towel and some softened margarine.

- To line round pans, place the pan on a sheet of parchment or waxed paper and trace around the pan with a pencil. Cut around the shape and you will find that this should fit the pan exactly.

- Deep, round pans for heavy fruitcake mixtures need to be double-lined around the base and sides. To do this, cut a piece of paper big enough to fold double and stand about 2 inches higher than the pan depth. Fold up the folded edge of the strip about 1 inch and snip with scissors along the folded piece in a slanting direction. Grease the pan and line the sides of the strip with the snipped edge at the base, lying flat. Place two rounds of paper on the base of the pan to cover the snipped edge.

- Parchment paper does not require greasing and is a very useful paper as mixtures, even sugary ones, will not stick to it.

Checking Cooked Cakes

- The last part of a cake to cook is the center, so after the baking time stated, check this area.

- For sponge cakes, press the center lightly with the fingertips. If the cake is cooked, it should spring back easily and not leave an imprint; the sides of a sponge cake should also shrink away slightly from the sides of the pan.

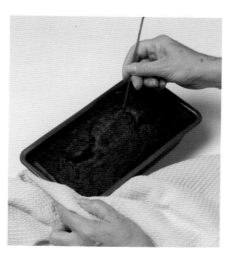

- To test creamed cakes or fruitcakes, insert a thin, warmed skewer into the deepest part of the cake. If the cake is cooked, it should come out perfectly clean, with no mixture sticking to it. If there is mixture on the skewer, bake the cake for a little longer.

- Small cakes should be golden, risen, and firm to the touch when pressed lightly in the center.

Cooling the Cakes

- All freshly baked cakes are very fragile, so I have given times to allow them to stand in the pans to cool to firm them.

- After the cakes are firm, loosen the sides with a palette knife if necessary, and turn them out to cool on a wire cake rack.

- Rich fruitcakes are very soft when newly cooked, so leave these in the pan for longer. Very rich fruitcakes, such as wedding cakes, should be left in the pans to cool completely to give a good shape to the edges.

- Peel away lining papers when the cakes are still warm, as they will then come away easily and keep the cake in good shape.

Storing Cakes

- Make sure cakes and cookies are completely cold before storing in an airtight container, otherwise condensation will form in the container and this can cause the cakes to go moldy.

- Store cookies in a separate container from cakes. Cakes have more moisture and will make the cookies go soft.

- Plastic food containers will encourage cakes to keep moist, so are ideal for richer sponge cakes, but an airtight cake container is necessary to keep cookies crisp and dry.

- Fatless sponge cakes, such as jelly rolls, will keep for only 1 or 2 days. Sponge cakes with added fat will store for 3 days, and richer cakes, such as creamed sponge cakes, will keep for up to a week.

- Light fruit cakes will store for 2 weeks in a cake container, but rich fruitcakes will keep for 1 month after cutting.

- Store undecorated, rich fruitcakes in their baking papers, prick the surface and brush with a little brandy or rum before storing.

- To store a rich fruitcake, overwrap in clean, parchment or waxed paper and seal with tape. Wrap in a double layer of aluminum foil and store in a cool, dry place.

- Store cakes with fresh cream fillings and decoration in the refrigerator.

- If you don't have a large cake container, invert a large mixing bowl over the cake on a plate or work surface. As long as the bowl meets the flat surface, the cake will stay fresh.

Freezing Cakes

- Each recipe gives individual freezer notes, but most cakes freeze well undecorated.

- Completely cool each cake and overwrap in strong freezer wrap or foil to exclude as much air as possible.

- To thaw, completely unwrap cakes and thaw at room temperature on wire cake racks, allowing plenty of time for larger cakes.

Basic Baking Ingredients

- Spoon measures are used throughout this book. Use the sets of plastic or metal measures sold specifically for this purpose and remember, all spoon measures should be level. Don't use kitchen tablespoons or teaspoons as the sizes of these differ and may be inaccurate.

Sugar

Sugar is added to cakes not just for sweetness, but also because it helps to produce a spongy texture and makes the cake tender. Always use the right type of sugar for the recipe.

- Superfine sugar comes in white and golden, unrefined varieties. It creams easily with fats and blends easily into light sponge mixtures.

- Light-brown sugar is grainy, and is often used for decorative toppings, or for recipes where sugar is dissolved over heat.

- Soft light- and dark-brown sugars cream well and are used in fruitcake recipes, or where richer colors and flavors are needed.

- Soft, dark-brown sugar, like muscavado, should be natural and unrefined, with an excellent, dark color and rich flavor for fruitcakes and gingerbreads.

- Granulated sugar comes in a coarse, white or golden, unrefined variety and is used for toppings as it does not dissolve easily in baking.

- Confectioner's sugar is white and powdery, but it also comes in a lovely, unrefined, golden variety. Store it in a dry place, as it tends to absorb moisture. Always sift confectioner's sugar before use, as it tends to forms lumps during storage.

Eggs

- Eggs should always be stored in the refrigerator, but you will get a better result if you allow them to stand at room temperature for 1-2 hours before using them for baking. Eggs at room temperature will whisk better and achieve more aeration.

- Don't use cold eggs straight from the fridge. If you are in a hurry, place them in a bowl and cover with warm water for 10 minutes to take away the chill.

- If you are separating egg whites for meringues, break them into a cup one at a time so that if there are any specs of yolk or pieces of shell in the cup, you can remove them easily.

- Sponge cakes and meringues will whisk up to a greater bulk if you use eggs that are over 5 days old.

- Eggs sold as economy or value eggs can be used for baking, but they may be ungraded and of different sizes, such as very small, or a variety of large and small. For best results, stick to eggs graded as small, medium, and large.

- Recipes containing raw eggs should not be eaten by babies, the very young, elderly people, or pregnant women. Dried egg whites give excellent results and can be substituted in royal-icing recipes.

Flour

Choosing the right flour for a recipe is vital.

- All-purpose flour provides the structure that makes the cake, but contains nothing to make a cake rise. Richer cakes and pastries that do not need leavening agents are made with all-purpose flour.

- Self-rising flour has leavening agents mixed into it that will make a cake rise. It is normally used for sponge cakes and light mixtures that contain no fruit.

- Bread flour is used for breads and cakes baked with yeast. This flour makes a dough that will stretch farther, to give a light, springy, open texture that contains air.

- Whole-wheat flour contains all the bran from the wheat, which gives a good texture, with extra fiber, and tends to keep cakes and breads moist. The nutty flavor of whole-wheat flour makes marvelous fruitcakes, breads, and pastries. You will need to add a little more liquid when using these flours, as the bran absorbs more fluids.

Leavening Agents

These make cakes rise when added to flour and produce a light texture. It is important to be accurate when measuring them out.

- Baking powder is a ready-made mixture of baking soda and cream of tartar. When liquid is added, the powder bubbles and produces carbon dioxide, which expands with the heat of the oven and gives the cake an airy texture.

- Baking soda is a gentler leavening agent and is often used to give spicy mixtures a lift. It must be measured accurately, as adding too much will give a bitter flavor.

- Cream of tartar is a fast-acting leavening agent that works the minute it touches liquid, so always bake the mixture as soon as possible after adding it.

- Self-rising flour contains baking powder. If you have only all-purpose flour available, add $2\frac{1}{2}$ teaspoons of baking powder to 1 cup all-purpose flour.

Fats

Fats give flavor and texture to cakes and improve their keeping qualities. Always use them at room temperature to make mixing easier.

- Butter and hard, block-type margarine can be interchanged in a recipe, but butter will always give a superior flavor, so don't stint for the sake of a few cents.

- Soft margarine is only suitable for all-in-one sponge-cake recipes, where all the ingredients are added and mixed together in one bowl. Don't overbeat these recipes or use soft margarine for recipes that require a lot of whisking or beating, as the mixture will become very wet and the cake will sink.

Dried Fruits

- Dried vine fruits are usually prewashed and cleaned when bought, but you may find large pieces of stalk in some packs, so it is worth picking them over. For rich fruitcakes, such as Christmas cakes, dried fruit benefits from soaking in alcohol, such as dark sherry, brandy, or rum, which will make the fruits plump and succulent. If you don't want to use alcohol, substitute orange juice instead.

- Candied and glacé fruits, such as cherries, and crystallized ginger and candied angelica, need to be rinsed and dried before use to wash away their sugary coating. If you don't do this, the fruits may sink to the bottom of the cake during baking.

Spices

Dried spices bring cakes alive. Although they have a fairly long shelf life, remember that they don't keep indefinitely.

- Spices gradually lose their aroma and flavor, so only buy in small quantities when you need them.

- Both light and heat affect the flavor of spices, so if you store them in clear glass jars, store these away from the light or keep them in a drawer.

- Store spices in a cool place, particularly if your kitchen is hot and steamy.

- Don't tip spices into mixtures straight from the jar as steam may get in and cause the spice to become damp and deteriorate.

Nuts

Nuts for baking can be an expensive purchase, and, as they deteriorate quickly, it is not advisable to buy them in large quantities. If you do have a large pack of nuts that you are not going to use immediately, store it in the freezer.

- Walnuts are very oily and will turn rancid quickly, so don't buy or store these in bulk. Just buy a small amount when you need them. Larger walnut halves are more expensive. If you need walnuts for chopping, buy cheaper walnut pieces, which are usually sold at budget prices.

- Almonds can be bought whole, blanched, slivered, sliced, or ground.

- Shelled almonds still have their skins on. If you need to remove these, place the nuts in boiling water for 2–3 minutes and you will find the nuts will slip out of the skins easily.

- Ground almonds have a fine, powdery texture. If you run out of ground almonds, place whole or sliced almonds in a food processor and work until fine. Be careful not to overblend them, as this will release the natural oils from the nuts.

Chocolate

Chocolate cakes are such a treat, so for a really professional finish and flavor, it is always advisable to buy the highest-quality chocolate you can find, although this will probably be the most expensive.

- The most expensive chocolate contains a higher percentage of real cocoa fat, which gives a flavor and texture that far outweighs cheaper varieties. The amount of cocoa fat or solids contained in a bar will be marked on the wrapper of any good-quality chocolate.

- If chocolate gets too hot during melting, or comes into contact with water or steam, it will seize or stiffen and become an unmanageable ball, instead of a melted mixture. You can add a little vegetable oil or margarine, a teaspoon at a time, to the mixture to make it liquid again.

- To melt chocolate successfully, break the bar into small pieces and place them in a heatproof bowl over a bowl of warm, not hot, water. Make sure the bowl containing the chocolate is completely dry and that steam cannot get into it, as steam and water are the enemy of melted chocolate. Heat the water very gently and leave the bowl to stand for about 10 minutes. If the water gets too hot, the chocolate will reach a high temperature and lose its sheen.

- The microwave oven is an ideal tool for melting chocolate. Break into pieces and place in a microwave-proof bowl and melt gently on low or defrost settings in small bursts of 1–2 minutes, checking and stirring in between.

- White chocolate is expensive and the most difficult to work with. It is best to grate it finely and keep the temperature very low when melting it.

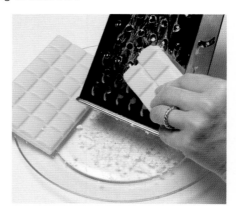

- Cocoa powder needs to be cooked for the full flavor to be released, so blend it with boiling water to make a paste before adding to a recipe.

- Drinking chocolate is not the same as cocoa powder as it contains milk powder and sugar, so don't substitute this for cocoa powder as it will spoil the flavor of a cake.

Extra Recipes for Decorating Cakes

Royal Icing

Royal icing is used to pipe decorations on to cakes, or to cover Christmas or wedding cakes to form a snowy, white surface.

Ingredients:

2 egg whites
2 cups confectioner's sugar, sifted
2 tsp lemon juice

1 Put the egg whites in a large bowl and whisk with a fork lightly until bubbling. Sift in half the confectioner's sugar with the lemon juice and beat well with a wooden spoon for about 10 minutes, until smooth.

2 Gradually, sift in the remaining confectioner's sugar and beat again until thick, smooth, and brilliant white.

3 Keep the frosting covered with a damp cloth until you are ready to use it. For piping, place in a small parchment-paper bag or cone.

4 To cover a cake, spread over the top and sides with a palette knife, then smooth down over the sides, or flick into points with the palette knife to make a snowy effect. Leave the frosting for 3 days to dry and become firm.

Almond Paste   *Makes 2 cups*

Almond paste is used to cover cakes that are going to be finished with royal icing or rollout fondant frosting. Almond paste protects and seals a cake and gives you the opportunity to fill in any cracks to make a perfectly flat surface before frosting.

Ingredients:

½ cup confectioner's sugar
½ cup superfine sugar
1 cup ground almonds
1 egg
1 tsp lemon juice
1 tbsp brandy

1 Stir the sugars and ground almonds together in a bowl. Whisk the egg, lemon juice, and brandy together and mix into the dry ingredients.

2 Knead until the paste is smooth. Wrap in plastic wrap and store in the refrigerator until needed.

Cook's Tip:

The paste can be made 2–3 days ahead of time, but after that, it will start to dry out and become difficult to handle.

Tips for Successful Cooking

- Use measuring spoons: 1 teaspoon (tsp) and 1 tablespoon (tbsp).

- All spoon measurements are level unless otherwise stated.

- All eggs are medium unless otherwise stated.

- Recipes using raw or lightly cooked eggs should not be given to babies, pregnant woman, the very old, or anyone suffering from, or recovering from, an illness.

- The cooking times are an approximate guide only. If you are using a convection oven, reduce the cooking time according to the manufacturer's instructions.

- Ovens should be preheated to the required temperature.

- Fruits and vegetables should be washed before use.

Pastry

Maple-syrup Tart

Family Favorite

I add grated apples to this traditional sticky tart, to help lower the sugar content. It is delicious served with spoonfuls of dairy custard dessert sauce.

Pastry:

1 cup all-purpose flour
¼ cup butter or margarine
¼ cup Crisco

Filling:

¾ cup maple syrup
¼ cup soft, light-brown
** sugar**
½ cup white breadcrumbs
½ cup dessert apple,
** peeled, cored, and**
** coarsely grated**
Finely grated rind and juice
** of 1 small lemon**

30 minutes preparation
25 minutes baking
Serves 6–8

1 Preheat the oven to 375°F and place a cookie sheet in the oven to heat. Grease a 9 inch pie plate or loose-based tart pan.

2 Sift the flour into a bowl and add the fat, cut into small cubes. Rub the fat into the flour with your fingertips, until the mixture resembles fine crumbs. Stir in 8 teaspoons of chilled water and mix to a soft dough. Wrap and chill for 15 minutes.

3 Cut away one-third of the pastry, then roll out the rest to line the dish. Trim away the edges and pinch into a decorative edge. Roll out trimmings with the reserved pastry to a long strip, about 10 inches long.

4 Cut into 8 thin strips and keep aside.

5 To make the filling, warm the syrup in a saucepan, then add all the remaining ingredients and stir well. Spoon into the pastry-lined dish and smooth level.

6 Twist the pastry strips and lay them across the filling in a lattice pattern. Press down the ends, then brush with milk. Place on the hot cookie sheet and bake for 25–30 minutes until the pastry is crisp and the filling is golden.

French Apple Tarts

Quick and Easy

If you need a superquick dessert, then rustle up these flaky, wafer-thin disks in under an hour. They are delicious served with scoops of vanilla ice cream.

Ingredients:

1½ cups puff pastry
4 large dessert apples
Finely grated rind and juice of ½ lemon
4 tsp golden granulated sugar
1¾ tbsp butter
2 tbsp apricot jam, sieved, warmed

20 minutes preparation
20 minutes baking
Serves 4

1 Preheat the oven to 425°F. Grease a cookie sheet, then dampen slightly with water. Peel and core the apples.

2 Roll the pastry out thinly, then cut out 4 6 inch circles using a saucer or small plate as a guide. Place the circles on the cookie sheet. Slice the apples as thinly as possible and toss in the lemon juice and rind.

3 Arrange the apple slices (overlapping) on top of each pastry in a spiral pattern. Sprinkle 1 teaspoon of sugar evenly over the apples on each tart.

4 Cut the butter into small pieces and dot over the apples. Bake for 15–20 minutes or until the apples are tender and the pastry is golden. Transfer to 4 serving plates and brush the top of each tart with warmed apricot glaze.

Cook's Tip:

- Sprinkling the cookie sheet with water will create steam during the baking and will help the pastry to rise.
- If you don't have apricot jam for the glaze, use thin-cut orange marmalade or honey instead.

Latticed Mince Pies

Easy Entertaining

Christmas would not be the same in Britain without mince pies and a glass of mulled wine. I make these well ahead of time, freeze them, and bake them when needed, so they are always piping hot.

Pastry:

- ½ cup all-purpose flour
- ½ cup self-rising flour
- ½ cup butter
- 1¾ tbsp vanilla-flavored superfine sugar
- 1 medium egg, beaten
- 2 tbsp milk

Filling:

- 1¾ cups best-quality fruit mincemeat
- 1 tbsp dark rum or brandy
- Confectioner's sugar to serve

25 minutes preparation

15 minutes baking

Serves 12

1 Preheat the oven to 350°F. Then grease a 12-cup muffin tin.

2 Sift the flours into a bowl and add the butter, cut into small cubes. Rub the fat into the flour until it forms fine crumbs. Stir in the sugar. Add enough egg and milk to bind into a soft dough. Knead until smooth, then wrap in plastic wrap and chill in the freezer for 5 minutes.

3 Roll out the pastry to a thickness of ⅛ inch. Cut out 12 circles using a 3 inch cookie cutter and press them into the cups in the muffin tin.

4 To make the filling, mix the rum or brandy into the mincemeat and fill each case three-quarters full. Gather up the trimmings and reroll into thin strips.

5 Place the strips in a lattice pattern over the fruit filling, dampen the edges, and press down. Bake for 15 minutes until the pastry is firm and golden. Dust with confectioner's sugar.

Cook's Tip:

Freeze the uncooked pies directly in the muffin tin, wrapped in aluminum foil. They keep for 3 months. To use, thaw thoroughly at room temperature, then bake as above.

Tarte au Citron

Freezer Friendly

I always serve this tart as a dinner-party dessert. Light and refreshing, it is ideal after a heavy main course, plus you can make it ahead and chill it until needed, so it couldn't be easier to serve.

35 minutes preparation

40 minutes baking

Serves 8

Pastry:

½ cup all-purpose flour
¼ cup butter
¼ cup vanilla-flavored
   superfine sugar
2 egg yolks

Filling:

2 lemons
4 eggs, beaten
³/₄ cup superfine sugar
²/₃ cup heavy cream

1 Grease a 9 inch tart pan. Put the flour and butter into a food processor or bowl and blend or rub in until the mixture resembles fine crumbs.

2 Add the sugar and egg yolks and mix to a soft dough. Pat the pastry into a circle large enough to line the pan.

3 Press into the pan, trim the edges, and prick all over with a fork. Chill the tart in the freezer for 10 minutes. Preheat the oven to 375°F.

4 Line the pastry with parchment paper and weigh down with pastry weights. Bake for 15 minutes until golden, then remove the weights and paper.

5 To make the filling, finely grate the rind and squeeze the juice from the lemons. Beat the eggs, sugar, and cream together until smooth. Pour into the pastry shell.

6 Reduce the oven temperature to 350°F. Bake for 40 minutes, or until set. Leave to cool in the pan, then chill. Serve with whipped cream.

Cook's Tip:

Cool and freeze in aluminum foil. Keeps for 2 months.

Raspberry & Apple Turnovers

Family Favorite

These flaky pastries are equally delicious made with blackberries or black currants, instead of the raspberries, when they are in season.

Pastry:

1 cup puff pastry
1 egg, beaten
1 tbsp granulated sugar

Filling:

1¼ cups cooking apples,
    peeled, cored, and
    chopped
¼ cup superfine sugar
1 tbsp butter
¾ cup raspberries

30 minutes preparation
20 minutes baking
Serves 4

1 Preheat the oven to 400°F. Grease two cookie sheets. To make the filling, put the apples, sugar, and butter into a pan with 1 tablespoon of cold water. Bring to a boil, then simmer for 5 minutes, stirring occasionally, until the apples are tender. Stir in the raspberries and spoon into a bowl to cool.

2 Roll out the pastry on a lightly floured surface to a 15 x 10 inch rectangle. Cut into six 5 inch squares with a sharp knife.

3 Divide the filling between the squares and dampen the edges of each square with water. Fold two opposite corners over to make a triangle. Pinch the edges to seal and press down with a fork to make a pattern.

4 Brush with a beaten egg and sprinkle the top with sugar. Place on the cookie sheets and bake for 20–25 minutes until puffy and light golden.

Cook's Tip:
Don't be tempted to overfill the pastries or the fruit filling may leak out.

Scotch Pies

Family Favorite

These tasty pies come from Scotland, where they are also called mutton pies. The pastry is made with oil, which means that it is easy to mold and supercrisp when baked.

Filling:

- 1 tbsp vegetable oil
- 1 small onion, finely chopped
- 1 cup lean ground lamb
- 1/2 lamb stock cube
- 1/4 tsp grated nutmeg
- A few drops of Worcestershire sauce or steak sauce

Pastry:

- 3/4 cup all-purpose flour
- 1/4 tsp salt
- 4 tbsp vegetable oil
- 2 tbsp milk, to glaze

45 minutes preparation
30 minutes baking
Makes 4 pies

1 To make the filling, heat the oil in a heavy-based pan. Add the onions and sauté for 2 minutes to soften. Add the lamb and cook until browned for about 5 minutes. Crumble in the stock cube, 4 tablespoons of water, and season with salt, pepper, nutmeg, and Worcestershire or steak sauce. Cook over a low heat for 5 minutes until most of the water evaporates. Remove from the heat.

2 Preheat the oven to 400°F. Grease a 4-cup muffin tin. Sift the flour and salt into a bowl and add the oil, along with 3 tablespoons of warm water. Mix to a soft dough and knead lightly.

3 Halve the dough and keep one half wrapped. Roll the other half out on a floured surface and cut out 4 x 6 inch rounds and use to line the muffin-tin cups. Roll out the remaining pastry and cut out 4 x 3 1/2 inch rounds for the lids.

4 Divide the filling between the cases, brush the edges with milk, and put the lids on top.

5 Seal and crimp the edges with thumb and forefinger. Make a hole in the center of each lid and brush with milk. Bake for about 30 minutes or until golden. Serve warm or cold.

Classic Quiche

Freezer Friendly

A warm slice of quiche with a plate of salad makes the ideal quick lunch or supper dish. This one freezes well and is a good standby for unexpected visitors.

Pastry:

½ cup all-purpose flour
¼ tsp salt
1³/₄ tbsp Crisco
1³/₄ tbsp margarine

Filling:

2 tsp vegetable oil
1 small onion, finely chopped
½ cup smoked, streaky
    bacon, trimmed, diced
⅓ cup Gruyère or sharp
    Cheddar cheese, grated
2 eggs, beaten
½ cup light cream
1 tsp French mustard

30 minutes preparation
35 minutes baking
Serves 4

1 Preheat the oven to 350°F. Grease an 8 inch tart pan. Sift the flour and salt into a bowl and rub in the Crisco until it resembles fine crumbs. Add enough cold water to bind into a soft dough. Roll out the pastry thinly to a circle large enough to line the tart pan.

2 Lift the pastry into the pan and prick the base with a fork. Chill for 15 minutes. Fill with parchment paper and pastry weights and bake blind for 15 minutes. Remove the paper and weights.

3 To make the filling, heat the oil and sauté the bacon and onion until the bacon is crisp and the fat runs from it. Scatter into the pastry shell with the cheese.

4 Whisk the eggs with the cream and mustard and season with salt and pepper. Pour into the pastry shell over the filling and bake for 30–35 minutes or until golden and firm in the center. Serve hot or cold with salad.

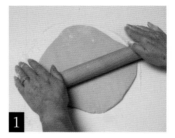

Cornish Pasties

Family Favorite

Cornish pasties are ideal for summer picnics. These ones have all the traditional Cornish ingredients, which keep the filling moist and tasty.

30 minutes preparation
40 minutes baking
Makes 6

Pastry:

2 cups pie pastry or pâte brisée
Beaten egg, to glaze

Filling:

³/₄ cup lean cube steak, finely chopped
¹/₃ cup potato, peeled and coarsely grated
¹/₃ cup rutabaga, peeled and coarsely grated
¹/₃ cup carrot, peeled and coarsely grated
¹/₃ cup onion, peeled and finely chopped
1 tbsp fresh parsley, chopped
A few drops of Worcestershire or steak sauce

1 Preheat the oven to 425°F. Lightly grease two cookie sheets. To make the filling, mix all the ingredients together in a large bowl, then season with salt, pepper, and a few drops of Worcestershire or steak sauce.

2 Roll the pastry out on to a lightly floured surface to ¹/₈ inch thickness. Using a saucer as a guide, cut out 6 x 6 inch rounds, rerolling the pastry as necessary.

3 Brush the edges of each round with a little beaten egg. Divide the filling into 6 and spoon into the center of each pastry round.

4 Carefully draw up the pastry edges to meet over the center of the filling. Bring the pastry together and seal the edges firmly.

5 Pinch the edges to make a fluted edge. Brush the pasties with beaten egg and place on the cookie sheets. Bake for 10 minutes, then reduce the temperature to 350°F and bake for a further 30 minutes until golden. Serve hot or cold with green salad.

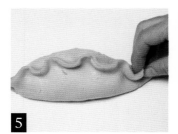

Apple Strudel

Easy Entertaining

These wafer-thin pastry layers are packed with a scrumptious apple filling and have a hint of chocolate.

Ingredients:

1½ cups cooking apples, peeled, cored, and thinly sliced
¼ cup superfine sugar
¼ cup mixed dried fruit
½ cup (five leaves) phyllo pastry
¼ cup butter, melted
1¾ tbsp white breadcrumbs
¼ cup dark chocolate, grated
Confectioner's sugar to dust

20 minutes preparation
30 minutes baking
Serves 6

1 Preheat the oven to 400°F. Grease a large cookie sheet. Mix the apples, sugar, and fruit together and then set aside.

2 Lay a leaf of phyllo pastry flat on a surface and brush with butter. Top with another pastry leaf and brush with butter. Make four layers of buttered pastry.

3 Sprinkle the breadcrumbs and chocolate down the center of the pastry and sprinkle over the fruit mixture.

4 Roll the strudel up to enclose the filling. Place on the cookie sheet, seam side down, and tuck in the ends. Brush the roll and the remaining phyllo leaf with butter, cut into strips, and arrange on top of the roll in loose folds.

5 Bake for 30 minutes until the pastry is crisp and golden. Serve with sifted confectioner's sugar.

Cook's Tip:

- If you don't have a large cookie sheet, bend the strudel round into a horseshoe shape to fit the pan.
- Keep the unused pastry covered with plastic wrap or a damp cloth until needed.

Flaky Tuna Slice

Family Favorite

This is another useful recipe for packing into lunch boxes. Alternatively, serve the slice piping hot with lots of green salad.

Pastry:

12oz pack frozen puff pastry, thawed
1 egg, beaten

Filling:

1 tsp vegetable oil
$^1/_2$ cup white mushrooms, sliced
1 small leek, sliced
1 stick celery, sliced
8oz can tuna, drained
1$^3/_4$ tbsp white breadcrumbs
$^1/_2$ cup mozzarella cheese, cubed

20 minutes preparation
30 minutes baking
Serves 6

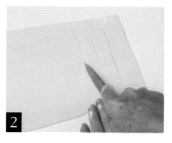

1 Preheat the oven to 425°F. Roll out the pastry to a 12 inch square, then cut the pastry square in half.

2 Lightly flour one pastry half and, using a sharp knife, cut a series of slits along the center to within 1/2 inch of the cut edge.

3 To make the filling, heat the oil in a pan and lightly sauté the vegetables for 5 minutes until softened. Cool in a bowl, then add the drained tuna, breadcrumbs, and cheese. Dampen a cookie sheet and place the plain pastry strip on the sheet.

4 Spread the filling to within 1 inch of the border. Place the slashed strip of pastry carefully over the filling to cover and match the edges. Dampen and seal the edges, then flute.

5 Brush the pastry with beaten egg and bake above the center of the oven for about 30 minutes.

Baking
with Yeast

Herby Dough Balls

Easy Entertaining

These light little rolls are so versatile. I serve them with hearty winter soups or bake a few trayfuls to serve with barbecues.

Ingredients:

1³/₄ cups bread flour
1 tsp salt
2 tbsp mixed dried herbs
1¹/₂ tsp dried packaged yeast
¹/₄ cup olive oil
³/₄ cup lukewarm water
1 tbsp melted butter

20 minutes preparation, 1 hour rising
20 minutes baking
Makes 16 rolls

1 Place the flour, salt, and herbs in a large bowl and stir in the dried yeast. Make a well in the middle and add the olive oil and water.

2 Mix to a soft dough. Knead for 10 minutes by hand or 5 minutes in a mixer with a bread hook. Knead until soft and smooth on a floured surface.

3 Divide in half, then divide each half into 8 pieces. Grease two 8 inch loose-based round pans.

4 Roll each piece into a smooth roll and place them in the pans. Leave enough space for the dough to expand. Cover with oiled plastic wrap and leave for 1 hour or until doubled in size.

5 Preheat the oven to 400°F. Brush the tops with melted butter and bake for 20 minutes until golden and springy.

Cook's Tip:

Add 1 crushed clove of garlic and 1 tablespoon of freshly chopped herbs to ¹/₄ cup melted butter and drizzle over the bread. Serve warm.

Cottage Loaf

Family Favorite

There's nothing to beat warm, crusty, homemade bread, straight from the oven. This old-fashioned loaf is great for serving with soups, or simply enjoy it sliced and buttered.

Ingredients:

- 1³/₄ **tbsp Crisco**
- **2 cups bread flour**
- **2 tsp salt**
- **2 tsp superfine sugar**
- 1¹/₂ **tsp dried packaged yeast**
- **1 tbsp salt**

15 minutes preparation
1 hour 30 minutes rising
30 minutes baking
Makes 1 loaf

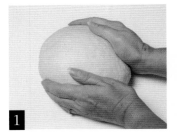

1 Cut the Crisco into small cubes. Stir the flour, salt, and sugar together in a bowl and rub the Crisco into the flour until it forms fine crumbs. Stir in the dried yeast and add 1¹/₄ cups lukewarm water. Mix to a soft dough, then turn out on to a floured surface and knead for about 10 minutes until smooth and elastic.

2 Return to the bowl and cover with plastic wrap. Leave in a warm place for 1 hour or until doubled in size. Knead the dough to knock out all the air.

3 Preheat the oven to 425°F and grease a cookie sheet.

Shape the dough into two balls, one using two-thirds of the dough, and a smaller one using one-third of the dough.

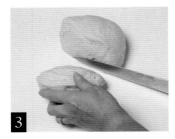

4 Place the large ball on the cookie sheet, then place the smaller one on top. Flour a wooden-spoon handle and use it to make a hole through the center of both balls.

5 Cover and leave to double in size for about 30 minutes. Dissolve the salt in 2 tablespoons of water and brush all over the bread. Sprinkle lightly with flour and bake for 30–35 minutes until the bread sounds hollow when tapped. Cool on a wire cake rack.

Pizza Base

Easy Entertaining

Everyone loves a pizza! This plain, white base is thin and crispy and you can try adding your own toppings and variations, too, all at a fraction of the cost of a bought one.

Base:
1 cup bread flour
1/2 tsp salt
1 3/4 tbsp margarine
2 tsp dried packaged yeast

Topping:
6 tbsp tomato pizza sauce
1 large beefsteak tomato, sliced
1 red bell pepper, sliced
1/4 cup salami, sliced

1/4 cup white mushrooms, sliced
1/2 cup artichoke hearts, sliced
1/4 cup canned anchovies, drained, sliced
1 3/4 tbsp black olives, sliced
1/4 cup mozzarella cheese, grated

30 minutes preparation, 1 hour rising
25 minutes baking
Serves 4

1 Sift the flour and salt into a large bowl and rub in the margarine until the mixture resembles fine crumbs. Stir in the dried yeast and 2/3 cup lukewarm water and mix to a soft dough.

2 Knead the dough for 5 minutes until soft and smooth. Return to the bowl, cover with plastic wrap, and leave for about 1 hour until doubled in size.

3 Preheat the oven to 425°F. Grease a large cookie sheet. Turn the dough out on to a floured surface and punch it to knock out the air. Knead until smooth, then roll out to a 12 inch round and place on the cookie sheet.

4 Spread the dough with tomato sauce and top with sliced tomatoes. Arrange the topping ingredients, then scatter with grated cheese.

5 Bake for 20–25 minutes until the base is crisp and the topping is golden and bubbling. Cut into wedges and serve immediately.

Sun-dried-tomato Bread

Vegetarian

Tomato bread is delicious served with cheeses and cold meats, or cut into strips and served with bowls of olives to accompany drinks.

Ingredients:

2½ cups bread flour
2 tsp salt
1½ tsp dried packaged yeast
5 tbsp olive oil
1¼ cups lukewarm water
1 tbsp coarse sea salt
1 cup sun-dried tomatoes, coarsely chopped

30 minutes preparation
1 hour rising
20 minutes baking
Makes 2 flat loaves

1 Put the flour in a bowl and stir in the salt and the dried yeast. Now add 4 tablespoons of olive oil with the lukewarm water and stir to make a soft dough.

2 Knead the dough by hand for 10 minutes, or in a mixer with a dough hook for 5 minutes until smooth and elastic. Cover in plastic wrap and leave for about 1 hour until doubled in size.

3 Turn the dough out on to a floured surface and punch it back to knock out all the air. Knead in the chopped tomatoes until evenly combined, then cut the dough in half.

4 Roll each piece out to an oblong measuring 8 inches x 6 inches. Grease two cookie sheets and place one dough piece on each. Brush with the remaining tablespoon of olive oil and make shallow, diamond-shaped slashes across the top with a sharp knife.

5 Preheat the oven to 425°F. Cover the dough with oiled plastic wrap and leave until doubled in size. Remove the wrap and sprinkle with sea salt. Bake for 20 minutes until the bread sounds hollow when tapped and is browned.

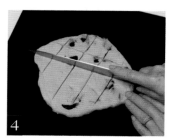

Grant Whole-wheat Loaf

No Fat

This whole-wheat bread was originated by Doris Grant, who was a health-food campaigner in the 1940s. This loaf is very easy to make as it needs only one rising.

Ingredients:

3 cups whole-wheat bread flour
1 tsp salt
1½ tsp dried packaged yeast
2 tsp molasses
2 tsp salt, to glaze

15 minutes preparation, 1 hour rising
25 minutes baking
Makes 1 loaf

1 Grease a 9 x 5 inch loaf pan. Mix together the flour and salt in a bowl. Sprinkle in the dried packaged yeast and continue to mix.

2 Make a well in the center of the flour and pour in the molasses and 1³/₄ cups of lukewarm water. Mix with a dough hook, or by hand, to make a soft, slightly wet, dough. Knead until the dough leaves the sides of the bowl clean and feels elastic.

3 Place the dough in the pan, cover with oiled plastic wrap, and leave to double in size for about 1 hour. Preheat the oven to 400°F.

4 Blend the salt with 2 tablespoons of water and brush over the top of the loaf. Bake for about 35 minutes. Test to see if the bread is cooked by tapping with the knuckles. The bread should sound hollow.

Cook's Tip:

Add your own topping: sprinkle the loaf with 1 tablespoon of cracked wheat, rolled oats, or poppy seeds.

Bread-dough Sausage Rolls

Party Special

This is a very economical way of making sausage rolls for a crowd. If you roll the dough thinly, you can make even more miniature sausage rolls.

1 hour preparation

25 minutes baking

Makes 32

Ingredients:

1³/4 tsp Crisco, diced
2 cups bread flour
2 tsp salt
2 tsp superfine sugar
1¹/2 tsp dried packaged
   yeast

2 cups pork sausage meat
1 tbsp tomato ketchup
1 tbsp mustard
A few drops Worcestershire
   or steak sauce
¹/4 cup mild orange cheese
1 egg, beaten

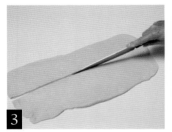

1 Stir the flour, salt, and sugar together in a bowl and rub the Crisco into the flour until it forms fine crumbs. Stir in the dried yeast and add 1¹/4 cups of lukewarm water. Mix to a soft dough and turn out on to a floured surface. Knead for 10 minutes until smooth.

2 Return to the bowl and cover with plastic wrap. Leave in a warm place for 1 hour or until doubled in size. Knead the dough to knock out all the air.

3 Preheat the oven to 425°F and grease two cookie sheets. Roll the dough into a rectangle 20 x 9 inches. Cut the dough in half lengthwise. Mix the mustard, ketchup, and sauce together and spread over the dough. Shape the sausage meat into 2 x 20 inch lengths.

4 Place one piece of sausage meat on each strip of dough, then sprinkle with the grated cheese. Roll the dough up around the filling and smooth each piece out, rolling gently with your palms.

5 Cut each roll into 16 pieces, slash with a knife, then brush with beaten egg. Place the rolls on the cookie sheets and leave to rise for 30 minutes. Bake for 25 minutes until golden and puffy.

Chelsea Buns

Easy Entertaining

15 minutes preparation
35 minutes rising
20 minutes baking
Makes 9

Ingredients:

1 cup all-purpose flour
½ tsp salt
1½ tsp dried packaged yeast
1¾ tbsp superfine sugar
½ cup milk
1 egg, beaten
1 tbsp butter, melted

Filling:

1 tbsp butter, melted
1¾ tbsp soft, light-brown sugar
½ tsp mixed spice
½ cup mixed dried fruit
2 tbsp maple syrup

1 Grease a 7 inch square pan. Stir the flour, salt, yeast, and sugar together. Stir the melted butter into the milk, beat in the egg, then pour into the flour and mix to a soft dough.

2 Turn the dough out on to a floured surface and knead until smooth for about 5 minutes. Roll out into a rectangle (12 x 9 inches) and brush with melted butter.

3 Scatter over the sugar, spice, and dried fruit. Roll up like a jelly roll from the longest side.

4 Cut the roll into 9 equal slices and place, cut side down, in the pan. Cover and leave to rise for 35 minutes until doubled in size.

5 Preheat the oven to 375°F. Bake for about 20 minutes or until light golden. Brush with maple syrup while the buns are still warm, then cool in the pan for 5 minutes. Turn out to cool on a wire cake rack, then pull the buns apart.

Cook's Tip:

If you don't have maple syrup available for a sticky glaze, dissolve together 2 tablespoons each of milk, water, and sugar. Simmer for 2 minutes and brush over the hot buns.

Hot Cross Buns

Family Favorite

Homemade hot cross buns are really special. If you are short on time, make the dough ahead and freeze it in the pan, ready to bake for breakfast on Easter Day, as in England.

Pastry:

2 cups bread flour
1/4 cup whole-wheat flour
1 tsp salt
1 tsp ground cinnamon
1 tsp ground nutmeg
1 tsp ground mixed spice
1/4 cup soft, dark-brown sugar
1 1/2 tsp dried packaged yeast
1/4 cup butter, melted
1 cup milk
1 egg, beaten
3/4 cup mixed dried fruit

Crosses:

1/3 cup pie pastry or
pâte brisée

Glaze:

1 egg, beaten
1/4 cup superfine sugar

40 minutes preparation
1 hour 30 minutes rising
25 minutes baking
Makes 12

1 Sift the flours, salt, and spices into a bowl. Stir in the sugar and yeast. Whisk the melted butter with the milk and the egg. Add to the bowl and mix to a soft dough. Knead for 5 minutes until smooth.

2 Knead in the fruit, then put the dough in a bowl and cover with lightly oiled plastic wrap. Leave in a warm place for about 1 hour until doubled in size.

3 Grease a large cookie sheet or meat baking pan. Cut the dough into 12 pieces and roll each one into a smooth ball. Space well apart in the pan. Cover and leave to double in size for about 30 minutes.

4 Preheat the oven to 400°F. Brush the buns with a beaten egg. Roll the pastry thinly and place a line along the buns, then repeat the other way to make crosses. Bake for 20–25 minutes until risen and golden.

5 Heat the sugar in 2 tablespoons of water until dissolved. Turn the buns out of the tray while still hot and brush the warm buns with the glaze.

Cinnamon Ring

Easy Entertaining

A slice of this sticky cake brightens up any lunch box.

Ingredients:

1¹/₂ cups all-purpose flour
¹/₂ tsp salt
1¹/₂ tsp dried packaged
    yeast
1³/₄ tbsp superfine sugar
1 tbsp butter, melted
¹/₂ cup milk
1 egg, beaten

Filling:

¹/₂ cup dried apricots,
    chopped
¹/₃ cup butter, softened
¹/₄ cup soft, light-brown
    sugar
1 tsp ground cinnamon
¹/₄ cup raisins
¹/₄ cup candied cherries
¹/₄ cup sliced almonds
2 tbsp honey

30 minutes preparation
1 hour rising
25 minutes baking
Serves 8

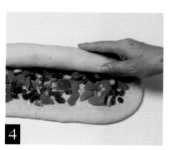

1 Stir the flour, salt, yeast, and sugar together in a bowl. Stir the melted butter into the milk, beat in the egg, then pour into the flour and mix to a soft dough.

2 Turn the dough out on to a floured surface and knead until smooth for about 5 minutes. Return to the bowl and cover with oiled plastic wrap. Leave until doubled in size.

3 Punch the air out of the dough and then roll out to a rectangle of 12 x 8¹/₂ inches. Spread with the softened butter, then mix the sugar and

cinnamon with the dried fruits and scatter over the surface.

4 Roll up from the long side, like a jelly roll.

5 Cut in half lengthwise and then twist the two halves together. Form into a ring. Place on a greased cookie sheet and cover with plastic wrap for 1 hour or until doubled in size.

6 Preheat the oven to 400°F. Bake for 25 minutes until golden. Brush with honey while still warm.

Cheesy Breadsticks

Easy Entertaining

Make your own crisp breadsticks to serve before an Italian meal. They are delicious served with dips and olives.

Ingredients:

1½ cups bread flour
½ cup whole-wheat bread flour
1¾ tbsp finely grated Parmesan or sharp Cheddar cheese
2 tsp salt
1½ tsp dried packaged yeast
⅓ cup olive oil
1 cup lukewarm water

To Finish:

1 egg, beaten
1 tbsp poppy seeds
1 tbsp sesame seeds
1¾ tbsp finely grated Parmesan or sharp Cheddar cheese

30 minutes preparation
1 hour rising
25 minutes baking
Makes 32 breadsticks

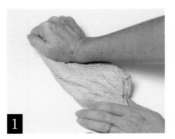

1 Place all the dough ingredients in a bowl and mix with a bread hook for 5 minutes to a soft dough. Alternately, mix by hand and knead for 10 minutes until soft and smooth.

2 Preheat the oven to 400°F. Grease two cookie sheets. Divide the dough into 32 strips ½ inch wide and about 10 inches long.

3 Roll the strips between the palms of your hands to make smooth, neat oblongs. Beat the egg with 1 tablespoon

of water and brush over each breadstick.

4 Place the sticks on the cookie sheets and sprinkle one-third with grated cheese, one-third with poppy seeds, and one-third with sesame seeds. Cover with oiled plastic wrap and leave until doubled in size for about 30 minutes.

5 Bake for about 15 minutes until crisp. Keep in a container or wrapped in aluminum foil until needed.

Fruit _{and} Nut Cakes

Irish Cake

Family Favorite

This dark, sticky fruitcake keeps moist for up to two weeks, so it's handy to have in a cake container to share with friends. Serve it sliced and buttered with a good, strong cup of tea

Ingredients:

¼ cup candied cherries, halved
1½ cups mixed dried fruit
Finely grated rind of 1 lemon
9 tbsp Guinness or stout
½ cup butter, softened
½ cup soft, dark-brown sugar
2 eggs, beaten
1 tbsp molasses
1 cup self-rising flour
1 tsp ground mixed spice
1 tbsp honey
1 tbsp light-brown sugar

10 minutes preparation
50 minutes baking
Serves 12

1 Place the cherries, fruit, and lemon rind in a saucepan with 8 tablespoons of Guinness or stout. Heat to just below boiling. Simmer for 3 minutes, then pour into a bowl and cool for 30 minutes.

2 Preheat the oven to 350°F. Grease and line the base of an 8 inch round pan. Place the butter and sugar in a bowl and beat until light and fluffy.

3 Whisk in the eggs, adding a little flour with each. Add the molasses, flour, spice, fruit, and 1 tablespoon of Guinness or stout. Stir together until the mixture is smooth.

4 Spoon into the pan, level the top, then make a dip in the center. Bake for about 50 minutes, until a skewer inserted into the center comes out cleanly. Leave in the pan for 10 minutes, then cool on a wire cake rack. Wrap in aluminum foil or store in a cake container for 2 days before eating. Brush the top with honey and sprinkle with sugar.

Rubbed-in Light Fruitcake

Family Favorite

This is a really easy cake for beginners to make. There is nothing complicated about it, and it always turns out light and even.

Ingredients:

1 large carrot
1 cup self-rising flour
½ tsp mixed spice
½ cup butter or margarine
¾ cup mixed dried fruit

½ cup soft, light-brown
** sugar**
2 eggs, beaten
3 tbsp milk
1 tbsp light-brown sugar

25 minutes preparation
55 minutes baking
Serves 8

1. Preheat the oven to 350°F. Grease a deep, 7 inch round pan and line the base with nonstick parchment paper.

2. Peel the carrot and grate it finely. Sift the flour and spice into a mixing bowl, add the butter or margarine, and cut it into small cubes.

3. Rub the fat into the flour with your fingertips until the mixture resembles fine breadcrumbs. Stir in the sugar, dried fruit, and grated carrot. Make a hollow in the center and add the beaten egg and

milk. Beat with a wooden spoon until it forms a soft, dropping consistency.

4. Spoon into the pan and smooth level. Make a dip in the center and bake for 45–55 minutes or until a warmed skewer inserted into the center comes out cleanly.

5. Leave in the pan for 5 minutes, then turn out to cool on a wire cake rack. Peel away the lining paper, then sprinkle with sugar and serve sliced.

Cook's Tip:

You'll need to use butter or hard margarine in this cake. Soft margarine will make the mixture too wet and the fruit may then sink.

Buttery Danish Almond Cake

Freezer Friendly

This buttery cake combines two interesting textures: a plain, light, and delicate sponge, with a delicious, crunchy, almond topping.

Ingredients:

½ cup butter or hard margarine
½ cup golden superfine sugar
1 tsp almond extract
1³/₄ tbsp ground almonds
1 tsp lemon juice
2 eggs
½ cup self-rising flour
1 tbsp milk
1³/₄ tbsp sliced almonds
1 tbsp confectioner's sugar

15 minutes preparation
40 minutes baking
Serves 8

1 Preheat the oven to 350°F. Grease a 7 inch round pan and line the base with nonstick parchment paper.

2 Beat the butter with the superfine sugar and the extract until light and fluffy, then beat in the ground almonds and lemon juice.

3 Beat in the eggs, a little at a time, then fold in the flour with the milk and mix until smooth. Spoon into the pan and smooth the top level.

4 Scatter with the sliced almonds. Sift the confectioner's sugar over the almonds and bake for 35–40 minutes until firm to the touch. Leave in the pan for 5 minutes, then cool on a wire cake rack.

Cook's Tip:

Add the beaten eggs in small batches, a little at a time. This will stop the mixture from separating or curdling, which will make the cake heavy.

Banana & Walnut Bread

Family Favorite

Banana bread is always popular, and is a great way to use up ripe bananas.

Ingredients:

1 cup self-rising flour
1/4 tsp baking soda
1/4 tsp salt
14oz ripe bananas in their skins
1 1/3 cups walnut pieces
1/3 cup butter or hard margarine
3/4 cup golden superfine sugar
2 eggs, beaten

10 minutes preparation
1 hour 15 minutes baking
Serves 8

1 Preheat the oven to 350°F. Grease and line the base of a 9 x 5 inch loaf pan.

2 Sift the flour, baking soda, and salt together. Peel the bananas and mash them with a fork until softened. Chop the walnuts coarsely on a board.

3 Beat the butter and sugar together until light and fluffy. Beat the eggs into the mixture a little at a time, adding a teaspoon of flour with each batch.

4 Fold in the mashed bananas, flour, and nuts and mix until smooth. Spoon into the pan and bake for 1 hour 15 minutes, or until a skewer inserted into the center comes out cleanly, with no mixture sticking to it.

5 Cool in the pan for 10 minutes, then turn out and peel away the lining paper. Store in an airtight container, or wrap tightly in aluminum foil.

Cook's Tip:

Don't buy walnut halves for this recipe, as these are expensive. Packets of mis-shaped walnut pieces are much cheaper.

Dundee Cake

Easy Entertaining

This long-keeping cake is ideal to make ahead for a special family tea, or as a guess-the-weight cake for a raffle. I think that it also makes a great New Year's present.

Ingredients:

1³/₄ cups mixed dried fruit
¹/₄ cup ground almonds
¹/₂ cup butter
¹/₂ cup golden superfine
　 sugar

Finely grated zest of 1 lemon
3 eggs, beaten
¹/₂ cup all-purpose flour
¹/₄ cup whole almonds,
　 skinned

30 minutes preparation
2 hours baking
Serves 8

1 Preheat the oven to 350°F. Grease and line the base and sides of a 7 inch round, deep pan.

2 Place the dried fruits in a bowl with the ground almonds and toss the fruit to coat it evenly.

3 Beat the butter and sugar and lemon zest together until light and fluffy. Whisk in the eggs, a little at a time, adding 1 teaspoon of flour with each addition.

4 Sift the remaining flour into the bowl and add the dried fruit. Fold together with 1 tablespoon of cold water until smooth and even.

5 Spoon the mixture into the pan, make a slight hollow in the center, then smooth level. Arrange the almonds over the surface in circles.

6 Bake for 1 hour, then reduce the heat to 300°F and bake for a further hour, or until a skewer inserted into the center comes out cleanly. Cool in the pan for 10 minutes, then turn out to cool on a wire cake rack.

Cook's Tip:
Store in an airtight container for a week to improve the flavor.

Fruity Gingerbread Loaf

spicy

These dark, sticky, gingery slices couldn't be easier to make. Just melt the mixture together in a saucepan.

Ingredients:

½ cup butter or hard
    margarine
½ cup dark-brown sugar
¼ cup molasses
¼ cup maple syrup
⅔ cup milk
¾ cup all-purpose flour
1 tsp ground cinnamon

1 tbsp ground ginger
1 tsp baking soda
2 eggs, beaten
⅓ cup golden raisins

Frosting:

½ lemon
½ cup confectioner's sugar
¼ cup unsalted butter, soft

25 minutes preparation
40 minutes baking
Serves 8

1 Preheat the oven to 350°F. Grease and line the base of a 9 x 5 inch loaf pan with nonstick parchment paper.

2 Put the butter, sugar, molasses, and maple syrup in a saucepan and heat gently until all the ingredients are melted and blended. Cool slightly, then whisk the milk into the warm ingredients.

3 Sift the flour, spices, and baking soda into a bowl and make a well in the center. Pour in the syrup mixture, then add the beaten eggs and whisk until smooth.

4 Add the golden raisins and pour the mixture into the prepared pan. The mixture will have the consistency of a batter. Bake for 40 minutes or until a skewer inserted into the center comes out cleanly.

5 Cool in the pan for 10 minutes, then turn out to cool on a wire cake rack.

6 To make the frosting, finely grate the zest from the lemon and squeeze out 1 tablespoon of juice. Beat the butter with the confectioner's sugar until light and fluffy, then add the lemon zest and juice. Finally, spread over the top of the cake.

Walnut Layer Cake

Easy Entertaining

This moist, nutty cake, layered with vanilla buttercream, is perfect for a special occasion. It's ideal if you are asked to make a cake for a neighborhood event.

Ingredients:

1 cup self-rising flour
1 tsp baking powder
1 cup soft margarine
1 cup soft, light-brown sugar
¹/₃ cup walnuts, finely
    chopped
4 eggs
1 tbsp molassess

Decoration:

¹/₃ cup unsalted butter
1 tsp vanilla extract
³/₄ cup confectioner's sugar
³/₄ cup fondant
    confectioner's sugar
Walnut halves to decorate

30 minutes preparation
25 minutes baking
Serves 12

1 Preheat the oven to 325°F. Grease and line the bases of 2 x 8 inch, deep, round pans with nonstick parchment paper. Sift the flour and baking powder into a bowl and add all the remaining cake ingredients.

2 Beat together for 2 minutes until smooth, then divide into the pans and spread level. Bake for 25–30 minutes until golden and springy to the touch. Turn out of the pans and cool on a wire cake rack. Cut each cake in half horizontally.

3 For the decoration, beat the butter, extract, and confectioner's sugar together until smooth. Spread thinly over one sponge-cake half and sandwich a layer on top. Continue layering the sponge cakes with the buttercream.

4 Place the cakes on a serving plate. Mix the fondant confectioner's sugar with 1–2 teaspoons of water to make a thin consistency. Spread over the top of the cake, allowing the frosting to drizzle down the sides. Place walnut halves in a circle on top.

Cook's Tip:

Freeze the layers sandwiched with buttercream, but undecorated. Keeps for 2 months.

Apricot & Marmalade Loaf

Freezer Friendly

20 minutes preparation
40 minutes baking
Serves 8

Ingredients:

1³/₄ tbsp orange marmalade
¹/₂ cup hard margarine
Finely grated zest and juice
  of 1 orange
1¹/₄ cup self-rising flour
¹/₂ cup soft, light-brown
  sugar
1 egg, beaten
¹/₂ cup dried apricots,
  chopped
1³/₄ tbsp dried cranberries

Topping:

¹/₂ cup confectioner's sugar
4 tsp fresh orange juice
1³/₄ tbsp each chopped
  apricots and cranberries
  to decorate

1 Preheat the oven to 350°F. Grease and line the base of a 8¹/₂ x 4¹/₂ x 2¹/₂ loaf pan.

2 Melt the marmalade with the margarine over a low heat, stirring until the fat melts. Remove from the heat and add the orange juice and zest. Cool for 5 minutes.

3 Place all the remaining ingredients except the fruit in a bowl and add the melted mixture. Beat together until smooth, then fold in the fruit. Spoon into the pan and bake

for 40 minutes until risen and firm in the center.

4 Cool in the pan for 5 minutes, then turn out to cool and peel away the lining paper.

5 To make the topping, blend the confectioner's sugar with the orange juice to make a smooth, runny frosting. Drizzle over the top of the cake, then scatter the center with chopped apricots and cranberries.

Cook's Tip:

Cool the cake and freeze undecorated for up to 3 months. Thaw at room temperature, then decorate with frosting.

Mincemeat Cake

Party Special

This is a great last-minute cake for celebrations, such as anniversaries or Christmas, and keeps well for 2 weeks.

Ingredients:

½ cup butter
½ cup soft, dark-brown sugar
3 eggs, beaten
1 cup self-rising flour
1 tsp mixed spice
14oz jar of fruit mincemeat
⅓ cup candied cherries
⅓ cup prunes, chopped
¼ cup walnut pieces, chopped
¼ cup dark chocolate, grated

Topping:

1¾ tbsp sieved apricot jam
½ cup candied or crystallized fruits, such as ginger, pineapple, apricots, cherries

35 minutes preparation
1 hour 45 minutes baking
Serves 12

1 Preheat the oven to 325°F. Grease and double-line the base and sides of an 8 inch round, deep pan with nonstick parchment paper.

2 Beat the butter and sugar together until light and fluffy, then add the egg a little at a time, using a little flour with each addition.

3 Sift the remaining flour and spice into the bowl, then fold in with all the remaining ingredients. Spoon into the pan, make a slight hollow in the center, and then spread the sides level.

4 Bake in the center of the oven for 1 hour 45 minutes to 2 hours. Test with a skewer—if it comes out cleanly, the cake is done. Cool the cake in the pan.

5 For the topping, brush the cake top with apricot glaze, place the candied fruits on top in an attractive pattern, and brush again with glaze.

Simnel Cake

Family Favorite

Traditionally in England, Simnel cake was made for Mothering Sunday, or Mother's Day, but it has now become a popular treat for Easter. Let the children add their own decorations, such as mini-Easter eggs and chicks.

Ingredients:

1 cup all-purpose flour
1 tsp baking powder
2 tsp mixed spice
³/₄ cup butter, softened
³/₄ cup soft, light-brown
    sugar
3 large eggs
2 cups mixed dried fruit

¹/₄ cup candied cherries,
    rinsed, halved
2 tbsp milk
Finely grated zest of 1
    lemon
2 cups almond paste
2 tbsp sieved apricot jam

45 minutes preparation
2 hours baking
Serves 10

1 Preheat the oven to 350°F. Grease and line a 7 inch, round, deep pan with nonstick parchment paper.

2 Sift the flour, baking powder, and spice together. Beat the butter with the sugar until light and fluffy, then gradually beat in the eggs one at a time, adding a little flour with each addition.

3 Add the fruit, milk, remaining flour, and lemon zest and stir until evenly combined. Roll out one-third of the almond paste to a disk the same size as the pan. Place half the cake mixture in the pan and put the almond-paste disk on top. Cover with the remainder of the cake mixture and smooth the top level. Bake for 2 hours or until the center is firm. Stand the cake in the pan for 5 minutes, then turn out to cool on a wire cake rack. When cold, brush the top with apricot glaze.

4 Roll out half the remaining almond paste to a round big enough to fit the top. Place on the cake and mark a criss-cross pattern on top and make a fluted edge. Roll the remaining paste into 11 balls and arrange on top of the cake in a ring. Toast the top of the cake lightly to make the tops of the balls light golden.

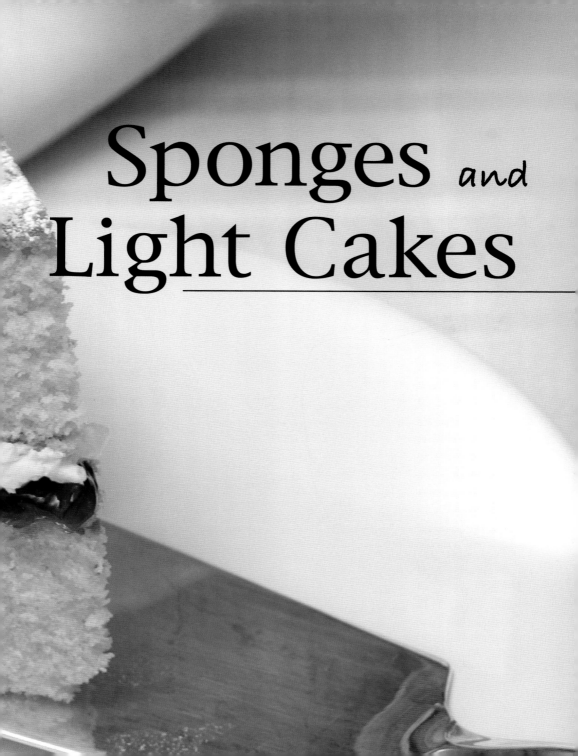

Sponges and Light Cakes

Cappuccino Coffee Cake

Quick and Easy

If you love coffee, then you'll really enjoy this light, fluffy cake. For a touch of extra luxury, try using a coffee liqueur, such as Tia Maria or Kaluha, instead of coffee extract.

Ingredients:

1 tsp instant-coffee granules
1/2 cup self-rising flour
1 3/4 tbsp cocoa powder
1 tsp baking powder
3/4 cup soft margarine
3/4 cup superfine sugar
3 eggs

Filling and Topping:

1 1/4 cup heavy cream
1 tbsp coffee extract
1 tbsp confectioner's sugar
**2 tbsp chocolate sprinkles
or cocoa powder**

20 minutes preparation
20 minutes baking
Serves 8

1 Preheat the oven to 375°F. Grease 2 x 8 inch round pans and line the bases with nonstick parchment paper. Dissolve the coffee in 1 tablespoon of boiling water and cool.

2 Sift the flour, cocoa, and baking powder into a large bowl. Add the margarine, sugar, eggs, and cold coffee. Beat together for about 2 minutes until the mixture is smooth.

3 Spoon into the tins and spread level. Bake for 20 minutes, or until risen and firm in the middle. Turn out to cool on a wire cake rack.

4 To make the filling and topping, whisk the cream until it forms soft peaks, then fold in the confectioner's sugar and coffee extract.

5 Spread half over the top of one cake and place the other layer on top. Spread with the remaining cream and scatter the chocolate sprinkles or cocoa powder on top just before serving.

Lemon Drizzle Squares

Family Favorite

These little sponge-cake squares are light and refreshing, and the lemon syrup keeps them wonderfully moist.

Ingredients:

¾ **cup butter or hard margarine, softened**
¾ **cup superfine sugar**
3 eggs, beaten
¾ **cup self-rising flour**
2 small lemons

Topping:

¼ **cup superfine sugar**
1 small lemon

15 minutes preparation
35 minutes baking
Serves 9

1 Preheat the oven to 350°F. Grease a 7 inch square pan and line the base with nonstick parchment paper.

2 Place the butter or margarine and sugar in a bowl. Add the eggs and sift in the flour. Now finely grate the zest from the 2 lemons into the bowl.

3 Beat together for about 2 minutes until the mixture is light and fluffy. Spoon into the pan and spread level. Bake for about 35–40 minutes until firm and golden. Cool in the pan.

4 To make the topping, cut the zest from the lemon into thin strips and put to one side. Squeeze the juice from the lemon into a small pan. Add the sugar and warm until it dissolves, then add the strips of zest and cool slightly. Spoon the syrup and the zest over the cake while still warm. Scatter with a little extra superfine sugar and cut into 9 squares.

Cook's Tip:

To freeze, cool the cake, top with the syrup, and freeze in the pan, wrapped in aluminum foil. Keeps for 2 months. To thaw, unwrap, take out of the pan, and defrost at room temperature for 2 hours.

Victoria Sponge

Easy Entertaining

In English tradition, no Sunday-afternoon tea would be complete without a proper Victoria sponge. You can make it with just a jam layer or just cream, but I prefer both!

Ingredients:

1 cup soft margarine
   or softened butter
1 cup superfine sugar
1 cup self-rising flour
1 tsp baking powder
4 eggs
1 tbsp milk

Filling:

4 tbsp raspberry jam
¹⁄₃ cup heavy cream,
   whipped
Superfine or confectioner's
   sugar for dusting

10 minutes preparation
25 minutes baking
Serves 8

1 Preheat the oven to 350°F. Grease 2 x 8 inch round pans and line the bases with nonstick parchment paper.

2 Place all the ingredients in a large bowl and beat together for 2 minutes until smooth. Divide the mixture between the pans and smooth it level.

3 Bake for about 25 minutes or until well risen and springy in the center. Cool in

the pans for 5 minutes, then turn out to cool on a wire cake rack. When cold, peel away the papers.

4 For the filling, spread one cake with jam and the underside of the other with cream. Sandwich together and sift superfine or confectioner's sugar over the top.

Cook's Tip:

To test if the cakes are baked, press the centers lightly with your finger, and the sponge cake should spring back.

Cherry & Coconut Slice

Family Favorite

It's always handy to have a nice, moist cake in the cake container. This one is an old favorite, full of sweet. coconut flavors and juicy cherries.

Ingredients:

½ cup candied cherries
1 cup self-rising flour
¾ cup softened butter or soft margarine
¾ cup natural superfine sugar
3 eggs
1 tbsp milk
¼ cup shredded coconut

15 minutes preparation
50 minutes baking
Serves 8

1 Preheat the oven to 350°F. Grease and line the base of a 9 x 5 inch loaf pan with nonstick parchment paper.

2 Wash the syrup from the cherries, dry them, then cut them in half. Place the flour, butter, and sugar in a bowl with the eggs.

3 Beat the mixture until smooth for about 2 minutes. Fold in the cherries and coconut with the milk.

4 Spoon into the loaf pan and smooth the top level. Bake for 50 minutes until the cake is risen, firm, and light golden. Insert a skewer into the middle and ensure that it comes out cleanly. Cool in the pan, then turn out to cool on a wire cake rack.

Cook's Tip:

Wrap and freeze the cake whole, or freeze leftover cut slices wrapped in aluminum foil for up to 2 months.

Seedcake

Family Favorite

Moist and spicy seedcake dates back to Victorian times, and was popular as a mid-morning delicacy. It was common in England for your bank manager to offer you a slice with a glass of Madeira. How times have changed!

Ingredients:

- **³/₄ cup butter, softened**
- **³/₄ cup superfine sugar**
- **3 eggs, beaten**
- **1³/₄ tbsp ground almonds**
- **1 tbsp caraway seeds**
- **³/₄ cup self-rising flour**

15 minutes preparation
40 minutes baking
Serves 8

1 Preheat the oven to 350°F. Grease and line the base of a 7 inch round pan.

2 Place the butter and sugar in a bowl and beat until light and fluffy. Add the eggs, a little at a time, beating well between each addition.

3 Stir the almonds, caraway seeds, and flour together and gently fold into the creamed mixture in the bowl.

4 Spoon into the prepared pan and smooth the top level. Bake for about 40 minutes until a skewer inserted into the center comes out cleanly. Cool in the pan for 5 minutes, then turn out on to a wire cake rack.

Cook's Tip:

Use the back of a wetted tablespoon to smooth the top of the cake mixture as this will slide around with ease.

Easy Orange Sponge

Quick and Easy

This recipe is easy enough for the kids to try. It will always rise well, and it doesn't matter if the frosting is not perfect. So, encourage them to start baking now.

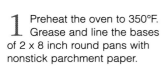

Ingredients:

1 large orange
³/₄ cup self-rising flour
1 tsp baking powder
³/₄ cup soft margarine
³/₄ cup superfine sugar
3 eggs

Filling and Topping:

4 tbsp orange marmalade
Half an orange
¹/₂ cup confectioner's sugar

15 minutes preparation
20 minutes baking
Serves 8

1 Preheat the oven to 350°F. Grease and line the bases of 2 x 8 inch round pans with nonstick parchment paper.

2 Finely grate the zest from the orange and squeeze out 1 tablespoon of juice. Sift the flour and baking powder into a bowl and add the orange zest, juice, and the remaining cake ingredients. Beat until smooth, then divide between the pans and smooth level.

3 Bake for 20 minutes until each cake springs back when pressed in the center. Cool in the pans for 5 minutes,

then transfer the cakes to a wire cake rack.

4 For the filling and topping, sandwich the cakes together with the marmalade. Cut long, thin shreds of zest from half an orange, then squeeze out the juice. Sift the confectioner's sugar into a bowl and add enough juice to make a runny frosting. Add a little orange coloring if preferred.

5 Smooth over the top of the cake, allowing some frosting to drizzle down the sides. Slice the zest finely and scatter over the top.

Cook's Tip:
Make a lemon version by substituting lemon rind and juice for the orange, and sandwiching the cake with lemon curd.

Honey, Ginger, & Lemon Gateau

spicy

30 minutes preparation

25 minutes baking

Serves 8

Ingredients:

½ cup honey
½ cup molasses
½ cup sunflower oil
½ cup soft, dark-brown
    sugar
½ cup milk
1 cup all-purpose flour
1 teaspoon ground ginger
1 egg
1 tsp baking soda
¼ cup crystallized ginger,
    drained and chopped

Frosting:

1 cup confectioner's sugar
½ cup unsalted butter,
    softened
2 lemons
Crystallized ginger

1 Grease 2 x 8 inch round pans and line the bases with nonstick parchment paper. Preheat the oven to 350°F.

2 Put the honey, molasses, oil, and sugar in a pan and heat gently to dissolve the sugar. Remove from the heat, then stir in the milk.

3 Sift the flour and ginger into a bowl. Stir in the egg. Whisk the baking soda into the melted mixture, then beat into the flour with a wooden spoon. Fold in the chopped ginger.

4 Divide between the pans and bake for about 25 minutes, or until the cakes are springy to the touch. Cool in the pans for 5 minutes, then turn out to cool on a wire cake rack.

5 To make the frosting, sift the confectioner's sugar into a bowl and gradually beat in the butter until fluffy and smooth. Finely grate the rind and squeeze in the juice from 1 lemon. Beat into the buttercream. Slice the remaining lemon thinly.

6 Use half of the frosting to sandwich the cakes together, then spread half the remainder over the top. Place the remaining cream in a pastry bag and pipe stars around the edge of the gateau. Decorate with lemon slices and ginger.

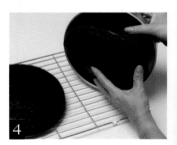

Coconut & Orange Cake

Family Favorite

This variation of carrot cake is coated in fluffy, white frosting and sweet coconut strands. The carrots and coconut make it a moist and long-keeping cake.

Ingredients:

- 1 cup butter or hard margarine
- 1 cup soft, light-brown sugar
- 4 eggs, beaten
- 1 cup all-purpose flour
- 2 tsp baking powder
- Finely grated rind of 1 orange
- 3/4 cup finely grated carrot
- 1/4 cup shredded coconut

Frosting:

- 3/4 cup Crisco
- 1 1/2 cups confectioner's sugar, sifted
- 2–3 tbsp milk
- 1/2 cup sweetened, shredded coconut

30 minutes preparation
1 hour 30 minutes baking
Serves 10

1 Preheat the oven to 350°F. Grease an 8 inch round, loose-based pan and then line the base with nonstick parchment paper.

2 Beat the Crisco and sugar together until pale and fluffy. Gradually beat in the eggs, adding 1 teaspoon of flour with each addition.

3 Sift in the flour and baking powder and fold in with the carrot and coconut. Spoon into the pan and make a hollow in the center. Bake for about 1 hour 30 minutes, or until well risen and firm in the center. Cool on a wire cake rack. Cut the cake in half horizontally.

4 To make the frosting, put the white fat and the confectioner's sugar in a bowl and then beat together with the milk.

5 Spread over the top and sides of the cake. Sprinkle with the sweetened coconut and place on a serving plate.

Jelly Roll

No-fat cake

A jelly roll is such a handy cake—make it from pantry ingredients in a morning ready for afternoon visitors. It contains no fat at all, so you can go crazy and serve it with spoonfuls of clotted cream and strawberries.

Ingredients:

3 large eggs
¹/₂ cup superfine sugar
¹/₂ cup all-purpose flour
6 tbsp seedless raspberry jam, warmed
Confectioner's sugar to dust

20 minutes preparation
10 minutes baking
Serves 8

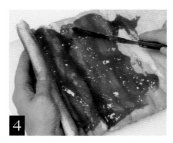

1 Preheat the oven to 400°F. Grease and line a 13 x 9 inch jelly-roll pan with a sheet of nonstick parchment paper, 2 inches larger than the pan. Snip the corners to fit.

2 Place the eggs and superfine sugar in a heatproof bowl and set over a pan of hot water. Whisk with an electric mixer until very thick and pale. The mixer should leave a trail when the beaters are lifted away. Remove from the pan and whisk until cold and thick.

3 Sift half the flour into the mixture and fold in carefully. Sift in the remaining flour and fold in with 1 tablespoon of warm water. Spread into the pan and smooth level into all the corners. Bake for 10 minutes, or until golden and firm to the touch.

4 While the sponge is baking, spread a dampened dish towel on a flat surface, lay a large sheet of nonstick parchment paper on top of this, and sprinkle with confectioner's sugar. Turn the cooked sponge out on to the sugared paper and trim away the crusty edges. Spread with the warmed jam.

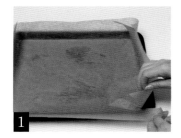

5 Roll up the sponge, using the paper as a guide. Leave the cake to cool wrapped up in the paper to prevent it from unrolling. To serve, remove the paper and dust with confectioner's sugar.

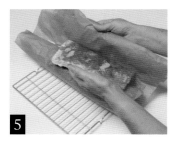

Orange Marble Cake

Easy Entertaining

This cake always looks impressive, but it really is quite simple to make. If you don't have a tube pan, use an 8 inch round pan instead.

1 hour preparation

50 minutes baking

Serves 8

Ingredients:

1 cup soft margarine
1 cup golden superfine sugar
4 eggs
1 cup self-rising flour
¹/₄ cup dark chocolate,
    melted
Finely grated zest and juice
    of 1 orange

Icing:

³/₄ cup dark chocolate
¹/₂ cup unsalted butter
¹/₄ cup white chocolate,
    melted

1 Preheat the oven to 350°F. Grease a 6-cup-capacity tube pan, then line it with thin strips of nonstick parchment paper.

2 Place the margarine, sugar, eggs, and flour in a bowl and beat together for about 2 minutes until smooth. Place half the mixture in a separate bowl and stir in the melted chocolate. Add the orange zest and juice to the other half.

3 Place alternate tablespoonfuls of the mixture in the pan and draw a knife through them to create a marbled effect. Bake for 50 minutes, or until a warmed skewer inserted into the center comes out cleanly.

4 Cool in the pan for 5 minutes, then turn out on to a wire cake rack and lift away the tube pan.

5 To make the frosting, break the chocolate into pieces and place in a bowl with the butter and 2 tablespoons of water. Place over a pan of warm water, or in the microwave, and melt together, stirring occasionally.

6 Pour the frosting over the cake, spreading it evenly around the top and sides. Leave it to set for 30 minutes. Place the white chocolate in a small parchment cone, snip away the end, and drizzle over the top.

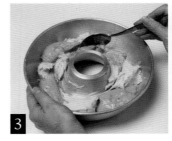

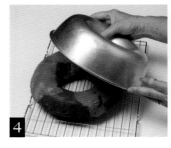

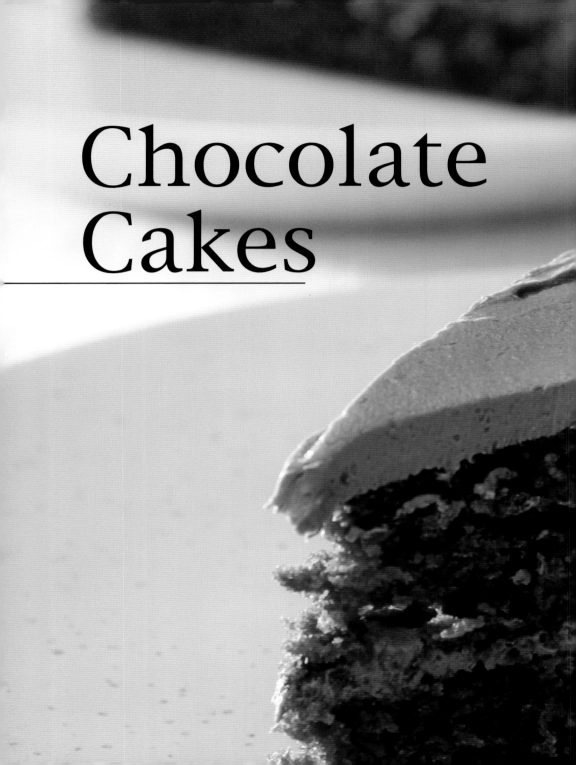

Chocolate
Cakes

Chocolate Fudge Cake

Easy Entertaining

30 minutes preparation

50 minutes baking

Serves 8–10

Ingredients:

3 tbsp cocoa powder
³/₄ cup all-purpose flour
2 tsp baking powder
³/₄ cup butter, softened
1 tsp vanilla extract
1 cup golden superfine sugar
3 eggs, beaten
¹/₂ cup dark chocolate,
melted
²/₃ cup sour cream

Fudge Frosting:

1 cup dark chocolate
1 cup heavy cream
Fresh strawberries to
decorate

1 Preheat the oven to 350°F. Grease and line the base and sides of a deep, 8 inch, round pan. Blend the cocoa to a paste with 4 tablespoons of boiling water. Sift the flour and baking powder together.

2 Beat the butter, vanilla, and sugar together in a large bowl until light and fluffy. Gradually beat in the eggs a little at a time. Fold in the flour with the cocoa mixture, melted chocolate, and sour cream.

3 Spoon the mixture into the pan and smooth it level. Make a slight hollow in the center to stop the cake from peaking. Bake for 50–55 minutes until a skewer inserted into the center comes out cleanly. Cool in the pan for 5 minutes, then move to a wire cake rack. When cold, cut in half horizontally.

4 To make the frosting, break up the chocolate and melt in a bowl over warm water, or in the microwave. Stir in the cream, beat until smooth, then cool. Whisk the frosting with an electric mixer until fluffy and light, chill for 15 minutes, then whisk again.

5 Spread a little frosting on one cake half, then sandwich the cake together. Spread the frosting over the top and sides of the cake. Decorate with strawberries to serve. Keep the cake refrigerated until needed.

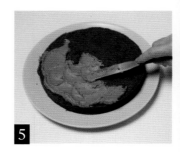

Brownies

Freezer Friendly

Brownies keep well in an airtight container for 4–5 days, but they do have a habit of disappearing—how long will they stay around in your house?

Ingredients:

- **½ cup butter or hard margarine**
- **1 tbsp cocoa powder**
- **¼ cup dark chocolate**
- **¾ cup dark-brown sugar**
- **2 eggs, beaten**
- **½ cup self-rising flour**
- **½ cup walnut pieces, chopped**

15 minutes preparation
35 minutes baking
Makes 12 squares

1 Preheat the oven to 350°F. Grease and line the base of an 8 inch, shallow, square pan with nonstick paper. Melt half of the butter with the cocoa and then add the chocolate, broken into pieces.

2 Remove from the heat and stir until the chocolate has melted, then put aside to cool. Beat the remaining butter with the sugar until light and fluffy.

3 Gradually beat in the eggs, then fold in the flour, nuts, and, finally, the cooled, melted mixture.

4 Spoon into the pan and spread the top level. Bake for about 35 minutes, until firm to the touch in the center.

5 Cool in the pan, then turn out. Finally, peel away the lining paper and cut into 12 small squares.

Cook's Tip:

To freeze, wrap the uncut block of cake tightly in aluminum foil and freeze. Keeps for 3 months.

Choc-chip Banana Loaf

Family Favorite

There's not too much washing dishes to do when you make this cake—it's all mixed together in a saucepan.

Ingredients:

³/₄ **cup hard margarine**
1 cup golden superfine sugar
10oz ripe bananas (before peeling)
1 tsp vanilla extract
1¹/₄ cups self-rising flour
1 tsp baking soda
3 eggs, beaten
¹/₂ cup milk-chocolate chips

20 minutes preparation
40–50 minutes baking
Serves 8

1 Preheat the oven to 350°F. Grease and line a 9 x 5 inch loaf pan.

2 Heat the margarine and sugar in a saucepan over a low heat until the sugar dissolves. Remove from the heat and cool for 5 minutes.

3 Peel and mash the bananas together with the vanilla extract. Sift the flour and baking soda into the pan with the melted mixture, then beat in the eggs and mashed bananas.

4 Fold in the chocolate chips, then spoon into the pan. Bake for 40–50 minutes, or until a skewer inserted into the center of the cake comes out cleanly. Leave to stand in the pan for 5 minutes, then turn out to cool on a wire cake rack. When cold, wrap in aluminum foil until needed.

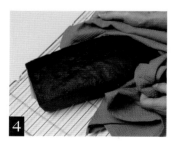

Cook's Tip:

The cake will form a crack across the top as it rises during baking, but don't worry, this is normal.

Chocolate Biscuit Round

Quick and Easy

This fluffy, chocolate biscuit cake is made in just minutes and sandwiched together with a tangy, orange-flavored buttercream. It's ideal for adding to lunch boxes.

Ingredients:

2 tbsp cocoa powder
1 cup all-purpose flour
2 tsp baking powder
⅓ cup butter or hard margarine, diced
⅓ cup soft, dark-brown sugar
5 tbsp milk
1 egg

Filling:

1 large orange
¼ cup unsalted butter, softened
½ cup confectioner's sugar
Orange food coloring

10 minutes preparation
15 minutes baking
Serves 8

1 Preheat the oven to 425°F. Lightly grease a cookie sheet. Sift the cocoa, flour, and baking powder together into a bowl.

2 Add the fat to the bowl and rub in with your fingertips until the mixture resembles fine crumbs. Stir in the sugar. Beat the egg with the milk. Pour into the bowl and mix to a soft dough.

3 Turn the dough on to a lightly floured surface and knead until smooth. Roll out to an 8 inch circle and place on the cookie sheet. Mark into 8 wedges and bake for 15

minutes until risen and firm. Lift the biscuit round on to a wire cake rack to cool.

4 To make the filling, grate the rind from the orange and squeeze out the juice. Beat the butter with the confectioner's sugar and mix in 3 tablespoons of juice and the rind. Add a little orange food coloring and beat until smooth.

5 Separate the biscuits and split each one in half. Spread with orange buttercream and sift a little confectioner's sugar over the top of each one.

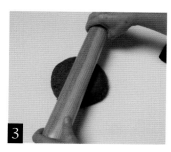

Chocolate-chip Cupcakes

Quick and Easy

These chocolate cupcakes are quick and easy to make. Let the children help to make and decorate them.

Ingredients:

¹/₂ cup butter, softened
¹/₂ cup soft, light-brown sugar
2 eggs
¹/₂ cup self-rising flour
1³/₄ tbsp cocoa
¹/₄ cup dark-chocolate chips

Frosting:

1³/₄ tbsp butter, melted
1³/₄ tbsp cocoa
1 tbsp milk
¹/₂ cup golden
    confectioner's sugar
¹/₄ cup milk-chocolate
    chips

25 minutes preparation
15 minutes baking
Makes 18

1 Preheat the oven to 375°F. Line an 18-cup muffin tin with aluminum foil or paper cupcake cases.

2 Sift the flour and cocoa into a bowl. Add the butter, sugar, and eggs. Beat until smooth, then stir in the chocolate chips.

3 Divide the mixture between the lined cups. Bake in the center of the oven for about 15 minutes, until the cakes spring back when lightly pressed. Remove them to a wire cake rack to cool.

4 To make the frosting, beat the butter with the cocoa, milk, and confectioner's sugar until smooth.

5 Spread over the tops of the cupcakes and sprinkle each one with a few chocolate chips. Leave to set for 30 minutes before serving.

Cook's Tip:

Fill the lined cups or cupcake cases only two-thirds full to allow the cupcakes to rise in a neat shape.

Classic Chocolate Profiteroles

Easy Entertaining

Profiteroles (cream puffs) make an easy supper-party dessert. I always bake the bases well ahead of time and store them in a container, then all that you need to do is fill them with cream and drizzle chocolate sauce over them just before serving.

Ingredients:

1/4 **cup butter**
1/4 **cup all-purpose flour,**
   sifted
1/4 **tsp salt**
2 eggs, beaten

Filling and Topping:

1 1/4 **cups heavy cream,**
   whipped
3/4 **cup dark chocolate,**
   melted

35 minutes preparation
20 minutes baking
Makes 18

1 Preheat the oven to 400°F. Grease 2 cookie sheets. Place 2/3 cup water in a heavy-based pan. Add the butter and bring to a boil.

2 Remove from the heat. Add the flour all at once and beat with a wooden spoon until a soft ball forms. Cool slightly, then whisk in the eggs, a little at a time, with an electric mixer, until the mixture is smooth and glossy.

3 Place 18 teaspoons of the mixture on the cookie sheets. Bake for 10 minutes, then increase the temperature to 425°F and bake for a further 10–15 minutes until crisp and golden. Remove to a wire cake rack and slit one side of each cream puff to allow any steam to escape. Then leave them to cool completely.

4 For the filling and topping, spoon the whipped cream into each cream puff, close the tops, then dip each top in the melted chocolate and serve at once.

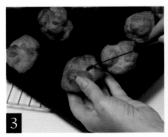

Cook's Tip:

Sprinkle a little water over the cookie sheet after greasing. This produces steam in the oven and helps the cream puffs to rise.

Carob Cake

Something Special

One of our friends can't eat chocolate as it gives her headaches, so I make this cake using carob, which tastes just as chocolately. You'll find it on sale in health-food stores.

Ingredients:

2 tbsp carob powder
1 cup soft margarine
1 cup soft, dark-brown sugar
4 eggs
1 tsp vanilla extract
1 cup self-rising flour

Filling:

15oz can crushed pineapple
1 cup whole-fat cream
**   cheese**
1 tbsp superfine sugar
1 cup fromage frais or
**   reduced-fat soft cheese**
3oz carob bar

50 minutes preparation
30 minutes baking
Serves 8

1 Preheat the oven to 350°F. Grease and line the bases of 2 x 8 inch round pans. Then mix the carob powder to a paste with 4 tablespoons of cold water.

2 Place all the remaining cake ingredients into a large bowl and add the carob paste. Beat together for about 2 minutes until light and fluffy. Spread into the pans and make a slight hollow in the centers.

3 Bake for 30–35 minutes until springy in the centers. Cool in the pans for 10 minutes, then cool on a wire cake rack.

4 To make the filling, drain the pineapple in a sieve and chop finely if there are any large pieces. Soften the cream cheese in a bowl, fold in the fromage frais or soft cheese, and then the sugar, then stir in the pineapple.

5 Sandwich the cake together with one-third of the filling, then spread the remainder over the top and sides. Grate the carob bar into large flakes and sprinkle over the cake.

Chocolate & Almond Cake

Freezer Friendly

This supermoist slice cake is simply packed with chocolate and covered in a gooey chocolate spread.

Ingredients:

- 1 cup dark chocolate, broken into pieces
- 1 cup butter
- 5 eggs
- 1/4 cup golden superfine sugar
- 1/2 cup self-rising flour
- 1/3 cup ground almonds

Frosting and Filling:

- 1 1/4 cups heavy cream
- 1/2 cup dark chocolate, broken into pieces
- A few drops of almond extract
- Chocolate curls to decorate

1 hour preparation
35 minutes baking
Serves 8

1. Preheat the oven to 325°F. Grease and line the base of a 9 inch square pan with nonstick parchment paper.

2. Place the chocolate in a bowl and add the butter, cut into small chunks. Melt over a pan of warm water, or in the microwave on low. Whisk the eggs and sugar together until thick. Sift the flour into the mixture and fold in with the ground almonds and the melted mixture.

3. Pour into the pan and bake for 35 minutes until firm and risen. Cool in the pan for 5 minutes, then turn out to cool on a wire cake rack. Trim the cake and cut in half.

4. To make the filling, heat half the cream until almost boiling, remove from the heat, and add the chocolate pieces. Stir until the chocolate melts, then pour into a bowl and beat until cool and thick.

5. Whip the remaining cream with the almond extract and use this to sandwich the cake together.

6. Spread the chocolate cream over the top and sides with a palette knife and decorate the top with chocolate curls.

Devil's Food Cake

Easy Entertaining

The beauty of the frosting on this dark, chocolate sponge cake is that it takes only 7 minutes to whip up. You'll need to swirl it on straightaway as it sets quickly.

Ingredients:

³/₄ cup all-purpose flour
1 tsp baking powder
¹/₂ tsp baking soda
¹/₄ cup cocoa powder
¹/₂ cup butter, softened
1 cup soft, dark-brown sugar
2 eggs, beaten
4 tbsp sour cream

Frosting:

2 large egg whites
1¹/₂ cups superfine sugar
¹/₄ tsp salt
¹/₄ tsp cream of tartar

50 minutes preparation
35 minutes baking
Serves 10

1 Preheat the oven to 350°F. Grease and line the bases of 2 x 8 inch round pans.

2 Sift the flour, baking powder, and baking soda together. Mix the cocoa to a smooth paste with 3 tablespoons of boiling water. Beat the butter and sugar together until light and fluffy.

3 Whisk in the eggs, sour cream, and cocoa mixture, then fold in the sifted flour and stir until smooth. Divide between the pans and smooth level. Bake for 35 minutes until firm to the touch. Cool for 5 minutes, then turn out to cool on a wire cake rack.

4 To make the frosting, place the egg whites, sugar, salt, cream of tartar, and 1 tablespoon of warm water in a large, heatproof bowl. Place the bowl over a pan of hot water and whisk, using an electric whisk, for 7 minutes, until the mixture is thick and white and stands in peaks.

5 Sandwich the cakes together with the frosting. Place the cake on a serving dish and swirl over the top and sides with a palette knife.

Chocolate & Strawberry Roulade

Party Special

I always make the base for this dessert cake the evening before I need it. It will become moist and gooey overnight, and all you need to do is to fill it with cream and fruit before you serve it.

Ingredients:

2 tsp instant-coffee granules
¹⁄₂ cup dark chocolate, melted
4 large eggs, separated
¹⁄₂ cup superfine sugar

Filling:

1¹⁄₄ cups whipping cream
¹⁄₂ cup strawberries, sliced
Confectioner's sugar for dusting

30 minutes preparation
15 minutes baking
Serves 6–8

1 Preheat the oven to 350°F. Grease and line an 11 x 13 inch jelly-roll pan with nonstick parchment paper. Blend the coffee to a smooth paste with 1 tablespoon of warm water.

2 Whisk the egg yolks and sugar together in a bowl over a pan of hot water until thick and pale. Remove from the heat and then stir in the cooled, melted chocolate and coffee mixture.

3 Whisk the egg whites until stiff, then fold 3 tablespoons into the chocolate mixture to loosen it. Fold in the remaining egg whites carefully.

4 Spread the mixture into the pan and bake for about 15 minutes, until the top is firm. Cool in the pan on a wire cake rack. Sprinkle a large sheet of waxed paper with confectioner's sugar and turn the cake out on to it. Peel away the lining paper and trim away the crusty edges of the cake.

5 For the filling, spread the roulade with cream and sliced strawberries and roll up the cake using the paper to help guide it. Serve sifted with confectioner's sugar.

Cook's Tip:

Roulades do tend to crack when rolled up, but don't worry, this just adds to their appeal!

Whole-whea
Goodies

Date Slices

Freezer Friendly

The evaporated milk in these chewy bars, combined with sticky dates, gives them a delicious, toffee flavor.

20 minutes preparation

25 minutes baking

Makes 12 slices

Ingredients:

- **³/₄ cup evaporated milk**
- **³/₄ cup pitted, dried dates, chopped**
- **¹/₂ cup butter or hard margarine**
- **¹/₃ cup golden superfine sugar**
- **1 tsp vanilla extract**
- **¹/₄ cup whole-wheat flour**
- **¹/₂ cup self-rising flour**
- **¹/₄ cup walnuts, chopped**
- **1 tbsp golden confectioner's sugar**

1 Preheat the oven to 350°F. Grease and line the base of a 7 x 11 inch, shallow pan. Place the evaporated milk and dates into a pan and cook over a low heat until just boiling, stirring well.

2 Pour the mixture into a bowl and mash the dates with a fork until the mixture is thick and sticky. Leave to cool for 15 minutes.

3 Meanwhile, beat the butter, sugar, and vanilla

extract together in a large bowl, until light and fluffy. Stir in the cooled date mixture and the flours, then stir in the chopped nuts. Spoon into the pan and spread level.

4 Bake for 25 minutes until firm and risen, then cool in the pan for 5 minutes. Turn out of the pan to cool on a wire cake rack. Dust with confectioner's sugar and, finally, cut into 12 slices with a sharp knife.

Cook's Tip:

Freeze the cooled cake without the confectioner's-sugar topping. Wrap in aluminum foil and freeze for up to 2 months.

Blue-cheese & Broccoli Tart

vegetarian

If you have a vegetarian to feed, this is a recipe that all the family can enjoy as well.

Pastry:

- **³/₄ cup whole-wheat flour**
- **¹/₃ cup margarine**
- **1³/₄ tbsp Parmesan cheese, finely grated**

Filling:

- **1 cup small broccoli florets**
- **¹/₂ cup carrots, thinly sliced**
- **¹/₂ cup blue cheese, crumbled**
- **¹/₄ cup mixed chopped nuts**
- **3 eggs**
- **1 cup milk**

30 minutes preparation
30 minutes baking
Serves 6–8

1 Preheat the oven to 400°F. Grease a 9 inch fluted tart dish and place on a cookie sheet. To make the pastry, place the flour in a bowl with the margarine and rub in until the mixture resembles fine crumbs. Stir in the grated Parmesan and about 2 tablespoons of cold water. Mix to a soft dough, then wrap and chill for 5 minutes.

2 Cook the carrots in boiling, salted water for 5 minutes and the broccoli for 2 minutes. Drain and refresh under cold, running water.

3 Roll out the pastry to a circle large enough to line the tart dish. Prick the base with a fork, line with waxed paper, and fill with pastry weights. Bake blind for 15 minutes. Remove the paper and weights and bake for another 5 minutes.

4 Layer the carrots and broccoli in the shell. Scatter the cheese over the top. Beat the eggs and milk together and pour into the tart. Top with the nuts and bake for about 30 minutes, until golden and firm in the center. Serve hot or cold.

Whole-wheat Carrot Cake

Freezer Friendly

There are many versions of carrot cake, or passion cake, as it is sometimes known. I like to use whole-wheat flour for this spicy cake as it helps to give it an extra moist texture.

Ingredients:

1 cup carrots
1 cup soft margarine
1 cup soft, light-brown sugar
4 eggs, beaten
1 cup whole-wheat flour
2 tsp baking powder
1 tsp ground cinnamon
¼ cup ground hazelnuts
⅓ cup golden raisins
2 tbsp milk

Frosting:

¾ cup whole-fat, soft
   cream cheese
¾ cup natural
   confectioner's sugar
1 tsp lemon juice

30 minutes preparation
1 hour 15 minutes baking
Serves 12

1 Preheat the oven to 350°F. Grease and line the base of an 8 inch, round, springform pan with nonstick parchment paper. Peel and finely grate the carrots.

2 Place the margarine, sugar, and eggs in a bowl and sift in the flour, cinnamon, and baking powder, adding any bran from the sieve.

3 Beat for 2 minutes, then stir in the carrots, hazelnuts, and golden raisins with enough milk to make a soft mixture. Spoon into the

pan and make a hollow in the center of the cake with the back of a metal spoon.

4 Bake for 1 hour 15 minutes, or until well risen and firm to the touch. Cool in the pan for 10 minutes, then turn out to cool on a wire cake rack. To make the frosting, beat the cream cheese, confectioner's sugar, and lemon juice together.

5 Spread the frosting over the top and sides of the cake in large swirls.

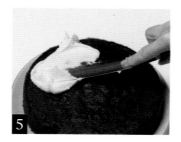

Gingerbread Cake

spicy

Spicy gingerbread is always a family favorite. Unlike other cakes, it does not dry out or go stale quickly, and it will become stickier the longer it is stored in a cake container.

Ingredients:

½ cup whole-wheat flour
¼ tsp salt
1 tsp ground ginger
1 tsp ground cinnamon
2 tsp baking powder
½ cup quick oats
¾ cup dark-brown sugar
6 tbsp molasses
½ cup hard margarine
1 egg, beaten
1¼ cup milk
½ cup raisins

20 minutes preparation
1 hour 15 minutes baking
Makes 16 slices

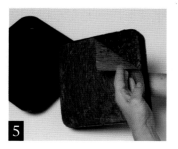

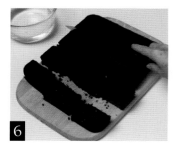

1 Preheat the oven to 350°F. Grease and line the base of a 9 inch square pan.

2 Sift the flour, salt, spices, and baking powder into a large bowl and stir in the oats and sugar.

3 Gently warm the molasses and margarine together in a saucepan until the fat has melted. Cool slightly.

4 Add to the flour mixture with the egg and milk. Add the raisins and mix together until smooth. The mixture will be very wet. Pour into the pan and bake in the center of the oven for about 1 hour 15 minutes, or until firm to the touch in the center.

5 Cool in the pan for 5 minutes, then turn out to cool on a wire cake rack. Peel away the lining paper while still warm.

6 When completely cold, store the gingerbread cake in an airtight container for 2 days to improve the flavor and texture. To serve, cut into 16 slices.

Date & Walnut Bread

Freezer Friendly

This plain, fruity bread is delicious served sliced and buttered.

Ingredients:

³/₄ cup dried, pitted black dates
¹/₄ cup walnut pieces
1 cup whole-wheat flour
1 tsp baking powder
¹/₃ cup soft margarine
¹/₃ cup soft, dark-brown sugar
1 tbsp maple syrup
2 eggs, beaten
2 tbsp milk

Glaze:

3 tbsp maple syrup or honey

20 minutes preparation
40 minutes baking
Serves 8

1 Preheat the oven to 375°F. Grease a 9 x 5 inch loaf pan and line the base with a strip of nonstick parchment paper. Chop the dates finely, then chop the walnut pieces into large chunks.

2 Place all the cake ingredients in a large bowl and beat them together with a wooden spoon for about 2 minutes, until smooth. If the mixture is dry, add more milk.

3 Spoon into the pan and bake for 40 minutes, or until a skewer inserted into the center comes out cleanly.

4 Cool in the pan for 5 minutes, then turn out on to a wire cake rack. While the cake is still warm, brush with warmed maple syrup or honey to glaze the cake.

Cook's Tip:

To freeze, cool and wrap in aluminum foil. Keeps frozen for up to 3 months.

Rolled-oat Crackers
Quick and Easy

Crunchy, rolled-oat crackers are the ideal partner to cheeses. You can buy commercially made ones, but these homemade ones have a nutty flavor and crunchy, crumbly texture.

Ingredients:

½ cup all-purpose flour
½ tsp salt
2 tsp baking powder
1 cup rolled oats
2 tsp superfine sugar
⅓ cup margarine
3 tbsp cold water

15 minutes preparation
15 minutes baking
Makes 28 rounds or 16 quartered circles

1 Preheat the oven to 350°F. Grease two cookie sheets. Sift the flour, salt, and baking powder into a bowl and stir in the rolled oats and sugar. Add the margarine and rub into the dry ingredients until the mixture resembles coarse crumbs.

2 Add enough water to make a dough of a firm consistency. Knead lightly on a surface sprinkled with flour.

3 Roll out to ¼ inch thickness and cut into rounds with a 2 inch round cookie cutter. Alternately, cut into 6 inch circles and then cut the circles into four quarters.

4 Bake for 15 minutes until light golden. Cool on the cookie sheets until firm, then lift off with a palette knife and cool on wire cake racks.

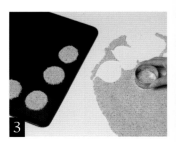

Cook's Tip:

When stored in an airtight container, the crackers will keep for up to 2 weeks. Freeze for up to 2 months. If they start to become soft, crisp them up under an aluminum-foil-lined hot grill for a few minutes before serving with cheese and butter.

Lemon Fig Rolls

Family Favorite

These sticky fig rolls are full of natural, whole-wheat goodness. The pastry is crisp and crunchy, the filling sticky and gooey, with a hint of lemon.

Ingredients:

- ½ cup soft margarine
- ¾ cup golden superfine sugar
- 1 egg
- 1¼ cups whole-wheat flour
- ½ tsp baking soda
- Finely grated rind of 1 lemon

Filling:

- 1 lemon
- 1 cup dried figs, chopped
- ⅓ cup light-brown sugar

40 minutes preparation
20 minutes baking
Makes 24

1 To make the pastry, beat the margarine and sugar together, then blend in the egg, flour, baking soda, and lemon rind with a fork. Form into a ball, wrap in plastic wrap, and chill for 30 minutes.

2 To make the filling, finely grate the zest from the lemon and squeeze out the juice. Place in a pan with the figs, sugar, and ⅔ cup water. Simmer for 20–30 minutes, until the mixture is thick and sticky. Cool.

3 Preheat the oven to 375°F. Grease two cookie sheets. Divide the dough into 4 pieces and roll each into a rectangle measuring 4 x 8 inches. Divide the fig paste into 4. Shape each piece into an 8 inch strip and lay down the center of each rectangle.

4 Dampen the seam side with a little water. Bring the pastry up over the fig paste to enclose it. Place seam side underneath. Cut each roll in half to form 8 rolls and place on a cookie sheet.

5 Bake the rolls in the center of the oven for 15–20 minutes until firm and browned. Cool slightly, then cut each roll in 3 with a sharp knife while still warm, then cool on a wire cake rack.

Mini-pizzas

vegetarian

These pizzas are handy for a quick summer lunch outside, or for a children's party. The uncooked dough can be made ahead and keeps in the freezer for up to 2 months.

Ingredients:

- 2³/₄ cups whole-wheat bread flour
- 1 tsp salt
- 1½ tsp dried packaged yeast
- 1 teaspoon soft, dark-brown sugar
- 2 tbsp vegetable oil
- 1½ cups lukewarm water

Topping:

- 12oz jar chunky tomato pizza sauce
- 2 bell peppers, sliced
- 1 cup white mushrooms, sliced
- 1¼ cup mozzarella cheese, thinly sliced

1 hour preparation
20 minutes baking
Makes 8

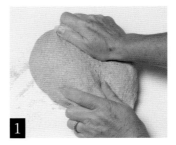

1 Mix the flour, salt, sugar, and yeast together. Whisk the oil and water together and stir into the flour. Mix to a soft dough, turn on to a floured surface, and knead for 10 minutes until smooth.

2 Return to the bowl. Cover with oiled plastic wrap and leave until doubled in size, for about 30 minutes. Turn out and punch the air out of the dough. Cut into 8 equal pieces and roll each one into a ball.

3 Preheat the oven to 425°F. Grease two cookie sheets. Roll each ball into a 5 inch circle and place them on the cookie sheets.

4 Spread each pizza base with 3 tablespoons of tomato sauce. Scatter the sliced peppers and the sliced mushrooms over the sauce, then top each with the sliced mozzarella cheese.

5 Leave for 15 minutes until the bases are puffy, then bake for 20 minutes until the bases are crisp and the topping is golden and bubbling. Serve immediately.

Vegetarian Biscuit Bake

vegetarian

35 minutes preparation

25 minutes baking

Serves 4

Cheese Sauce:

1 tbsp margarine
1 tbsp all-purpose flour
1¼ cups milk
⅓ cup Cheddar cheese,
finely grated

Filling:

1 cup celery, thinly sliced
1 cup carrots, thinly sliced
½ cup white mushrooms,
quartered
14oz can cannellini beans,
drained

Topping:

1 cup whole-wheat flour
2 tsp baking powder
½ tsp baking soda
¼ tsp salt
⅓ cup margarine
⅔ cup milk
3 tbsp plain yogurt

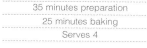

1 To make the sauce, melt the fat in a saucepan and stir in the flour. Cook for 1 minute over a gentle heat. Gradually whisk in the milk and bring to a boil, stirring all the time. Simmer for 3 minutes, then add the cheese and stir until melted and blended.

2 Preheat the oven to 400°F. Grease a shallow, 6½-cup-capacity, ovenproof dish. Add the sliced vegetables and beans to the sauce and spoon into the base of the dish.

3 To make the topping, sift the flour with the baking powder, baking soda, and salt. Add the margarine, cut into small pieces, and rub into the flour until the mixture resembles fine crumbs. Stir in the milk and yogurt to make a soft dough and then knead until smooth.

4 Roll out the dough and cut out 12 rounds with a 2½ inch round cookie cutter. Place the rounds on top of the vegetables, overlapping them and leaving the center open. Brush the biscuits with a little milk and bake for 20–25 minutes, until the scones are risen and golden and the filling is hot and bubbling. Serve immediately.

Soda Bread

Reduced Fat

If you run out of bread over a busy weekend, don't worry. Just bake this easy, yeast-free bread and serve it within the hour. It is delicious served warm, and is meant to be eaten on the day of baking.

Ingredients:

1 cup all-purpose flour
1½ cups whole-wheat flour
1 tsp salt
1 tsp baking soda
1 tbsp baking powder
1 tsp vegetable oil
⅔ cup plain yogurt or buttermilk
⅔ cup cold water

15 minutes preparation
30 minutes baking
Makes 2 loaves

1 Preheat the oven to 400°F. Grease a cookie sheet and dust it with flour.

2 Sift the flours, salt, baking soda, and baking powder into a bowl and add the bran from the sieve to the bowl.

3 Mix the oil and yogurt together with a fork and add to the bowl with the water. Mix to a soft dough, then turn out on to a floured surface and knead until smooth.

4 Divide into 2 pieces and roll each into a ball.

5 With a sharp knife, cut a deep cross in the middle of each round. Place on the cookie sheets and dust each one with flour. Bake for 30 minutes until crisp and browned. Cool for 10 minutes, then break the bread into quarters to serve.

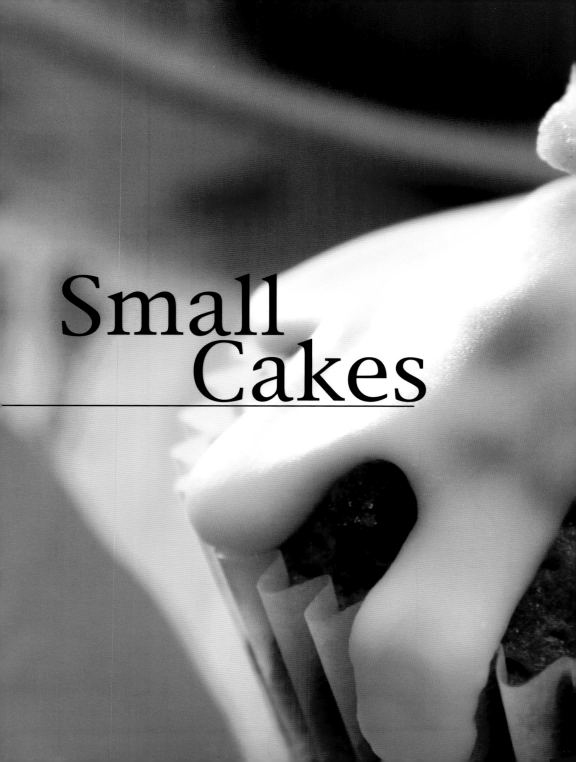

Small
Cakes

Quick Butterfly Cakes

Quick and Easy

These traditional teatime favorites are easy to make. Get the kids to make them using different colored frostings.

Ingredients:

½ cup soft margarine
½ cup superfine sugar
2 eggs
½ cup self-rising flour
1 tsp baking powder
1 tsp vanilla extract

Frosting:

½ cup unsalted butter, soft
**1 cup confectioner's sugar,
 sifted**
½ tsp vanilla extract
Pink food coloring
**Confectioner's sugar for
 dusting**

30 minutes preparation
15–20 minutes baking
Makes 12–14

1 Preheat the oven to 400°F. Line a muffin tin with 12 muffin liners.

2 Place all the cake ingredients in a large bowl and beat with an electric mixer for about 2 minutes until smooth. Half-fill the muffin liners with the mixture.

3 Bake for 15 minutes or until the cakes are risen and golden. Remove from the muffin tin and cool on a wire cake rack.

4 To make the frosting, beat together the butter, confectioner's sugar, coloring, and extract until smooth.

5 Cut a slice from the top of each cake, then cut in half to form wings. Pipe or spoon on a little buttercream and replace the halves at an angle to form butterfly wings. Dust with confectioner's sugar before serving.

Cook's Tip:

Bake the cakes and make the buttercream ahead of time and freeze separately. Defrost and decorate when needed.

Cherry Berry Muffins

Quick and Easy

If you have weekend visitors, make and serve these muffins for breakfast. They are at their best when eaten warm, straight from the oven.

Ingredients:

1 cup all-purpose flour
1 tsp baking powder
¹/₂ tsp baking soda
¹/₄ cup superfine sugar
1 egg
1 cup milk
¹/₄ cup butter, melted and cooled
¹/₄ cup red candied cherries, washed and quartered
³/₄ cup raspberries, part-thawed if frozen
¹/₄ cup dried cranberries
Finely grated rind of ¹/₂ orange or lemon

10 minutes preparation
20 minutes baking
Makes 10

1 Preheat the oven to 400°F. Place 10 large muffin liners in a muffin tin with deep cups.

2 Sift all the dry ingredients into a bowl and make a well in the center. Beat the egg and milk together and add to the dry ingredients. Finally, add the melted butter.

3 Beat the mixture lightly with a fork until all the flour is combined, but the mixture remains slightly lumpy. Fold in the fruit and rind and spoon into the muffin liners.

4 Bake for about 20 minutes, or until a skewer inserted in the middle comes out cleanly. Serve warm or cold. Must be eaten on the same day as baking.

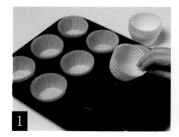

Cook's Tip:

Don't be tempted to overbeat the mixture until smooth as this makes the muffins go flat.

Fruity Biscuits

Family Favorite

Old-fashioned fruit biscuits (or English scones) are delicious served split and buttered. These ones can be made and baked in under half an hour.

15 minutes preparation
10–15 minutes baking
Makes 9

Ingredients:

1 cup self-rising flour
1 tsp baking powder
¼ cup butter
1¾ tsp golden superfine sugar
⅓ cup mixed dried fruit
1¾ tsp walnuts, chopped
1 egg
Just under ⅔ cup milk

1 Preheat the oven to 425°F. Grease two cookie sheets.

2 Sift the flour and baking powder into a bowl, add the butter, and rub in until the mixture resembles fine crumbs. Stir in the sugar and fruit.

3 Break the egg into a measuring container and bring the level up to ⅔ cup with milk. Beat and stir into the dry ingredients to make a soft dough. Place on a lightly floured surface and knead lightly until smooth.

4 Roll out the dough and cut into 9 2 inch rounds. Place on the cookie sheets, brush the tops with milk, and bake for 10 minutes or until golden. Cool and then serve spilt in half and buttered.

Cook's tip:

• Dip the cutter into flour before cutting out the rounds.
• The dough should be soft and spongy. Handle very lightly for the best results.

Choc Rock Cakes

Quick and Easy

Making little rock cakes, as these biscuits are called in England, is an ideal way to introduce the kids to baking.

15 minutes preparation

12 minutes baking

Makes 14 small cakes

Ingredients:

1 cup self-rising flour
¼ tsp salt
⅓ cup butter or hard margarine
1 tbsp superfine sugar
1 egg, beaten
4–5 tbsp milk
½ cup chocolate chips
2 tbsp light-brown sugar

1 Preheat the oven to 400°F. Then lightly grease two cookie sheets.

2 Sift the flour and salt into a bowl and add the butter, cut into pieces. Rub in the fat until the mixture resembles fine crumbs. Stir in the sugar.

3 Add the egg and enough milk to make a soft mixture. Lightly knead in the chocolate chips.

4 Shape into 12–14 small heaps and place on the cookie sheets. Bake for 12–15 minutes until firm and golden brown. Cool and sprinkle with sugar.

Cook's Tip:

- Rock cakes are best eaten on the day of baking.
- For a variation, add ½ cup mixed dried fruit or chopped walnuts instead of chocolate chips.

Palmiers

The secret to making these heart-shaped pastries is in the folding of the pastry. Follow the instructions to make these light-as-air delicacies.

Ingredients:

1lb packet puff pastry, thawed if frozen
³/₄ cup light-brown sugar

Filling:

²/₃ cup heavy cream
1 tsp superfine sugar
A few drops vanilla extract
1 cup fresh strawberries, halved

45 minutes preparation
20 minutes baking
Makes 12

1 Preheat the oven to 400°F. Cut the puff pastry in half. Scatter a working surface with ¹/₄ cup light-brown sugar and roll half the pastry into a rectangle measuring 12 x 10 inches. Trim to form straight edges and corners.

2 Fold the two long pastry edges over to meet in the center. Lightly sprinkle the top with another 1³/₄ tablespoon of sugar, then take one side of the pastry and fold it over to cover the other half.

3 With a sharp knife, cut the folded pastry strip into 12 narrow slices ¹/₂ inch wide. Repeat the whole rolling and folding process with the other half of the pastry, then chill until needed.

4 Dampen a cookie sheet and place 6 palmiers on the sheet, allowing room for them to spread. Pinch the joined end of each pastry together, then flatten out with the heels of your hands.

5 Bake the pastries toward the top of the oven for 15–20 minutes until light golden brown and the sugar on the outside has turned to caramel. Bake the remaining pastries in the same way.

6 For the filling, whip the cream until stiff, then fold in the vanilla extract and sugar. Place in a pastry bag fitted with a star nozzle and pipe a heart on each pastry. Sandwich a plain pastry on top, pipe on a swirl of cream, and finally decorate with a strawberry half.

Macaroons

No Fat

Light as air, macaroons have a delicious, soft, almond filling. Serve them with coffee or to accompany desserts.

Ingredients:

Rice-paper sheets
½ cup ground almonds
¾ cup superfine sugar
2 egg whites
A few drops of almond extract

Decoration:

16 almond halves
Egg white to glaze
Superfine sugar to sprinkle

15 minutes preparation
15 minutes baking
Makes 16

1 Preheat the oven to 350°F. Line two cookie sheets with rice-paper sheets.

2 Stir the almonds and sugar together. Whisk the egg whites with the almond extract until stiff.

3 Gradually beat in the almonds and sugar until the mixture is a stiff paste. Spoon into a large pastry bag fitted with a plain nozzle.

4 Pipe 16 small rounds on to the rice paper, spacing them well apart. For the decoration, whisk the egg white lightly and brush over each round. Sprinkle lightly with superfine sugar.

5 Press a halved almond into the center of each round and bake for about 15 minutes, or until the macaroons are just beginning to become pale golden. Cool on the cookie sheets until firm, then break away the rice paper to separate the cakes.

Cook's Tip:

Store the macaroons in an airtight container to keep them crisp and dry for up to 1 week. Don't use a plastic storage box as this will encourage them to become moist and soft.

Mini-meringues
Easy Entertaining

For a special afternoon tea, make these delicious, crisp delicacies.

Ingredients:

1/3 cup superfine sugar
1/3 cup golden superfine
    sugar
3 egg whites
1/4 tsp cream of tartar

Filling:

1/2 cup dark chocolate
2/3 cup heavy cream

30 minutes preparation
1 1/2 hours baking
Makes 15 double meringues

1 Preheat the oven to 225°F. Line two cookie sheets with nonstick parchment paper. Stir the sugars together.

2 Place the egg whites in a clean, dry, grease-free bowl and whisk with the cream of tartar until they are stiff.

3 Whisk in the sugar, a little at a time, making sure that the meringue is stiff before the next addition.

4 Place the meringue in a pastry bag fitted with a star nozzle. Pipe 30 small rounds on the paper. Bake for about 1 1/2 hours, or until crisp

and dry. Reverse the sheets halfway through the baking.

5 Leave to cool on a wire cake rack on the paper and slide away the paper when cold.

6 To make the filling, melt the chocolate in a bowl over a pan of warm water, or in the microwave on low. Dip the underside of each meringue in the chocolate and leave to dry on nonstick parchment paper. Whip the cream and sandwich the meringues together in pairs. Place in paper cases to serve.

Cook's Tip:

Make the meringue bases ahead of time and store them, undecorated, in an airtight container for up to 3 days. Then dip in the chocolate and sandwich with cream just before serving.

Banana Fudge Muffins

Family Favorite

These moist, banana muffins contain mini-pieces of fudge, with a toffee-flavored frosting. They don't last long in our household!

Ingredients:

6oz ripe bananas
1/2 cup soft margarine
1/3 cup soft, light-brown sugar
1/4 cup soft caramel fudge
2 eggs
1 tbsp milk
1 cup all-purpose flour
1 tsp baking powder

Topping:

1/2 cup golden, unrefined confectioner's sugar
1/2 tsp butterscotch extract
10 dried banana chips

15 minutes preparation
20 minutes baking
Makes 10 large cakes

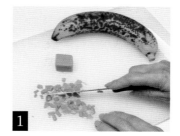

1 Preheat the oven to 350°F. Place 10 large muffin liners in deep muffin tins. Peel the bananas and mash the fruit in a bowl. Chop the fudge into small cubes.

2 Add the margarine, sugar, eggs, and milk to the bowl with the bananas, then sift in the flour and baking powder. Beat together for 2 minutes until smooth. Stir in the fudge.

3 Divide between the muffin liners. Bake for 20–25 minutes until a skewer inserted comes out cleanly. Cool on a wire cake rack.

4 For the topping, blend the confectioner's sugar with the extract and 4 teaspoons of cold water and mix to a thin glace icing. Spoon over the top of each cake, then top each one with a banana chip.

Cook's Tip:

If you don't have deep muffin tins, bake the mixture in 24 small muffin liners on cookie sheets for 15 minutes.

Pink Piggies

Party Special

Little cakes with an animal theme are always popular for children's parties. Why not get the kids to help you decorate them?

Ingredients:

½ cup soft margarine
½ cup superfine sugar
2 eggs
½ cup self-rising flour
A few drops of vanilla
   extract

Decoration:

Pink food coloring
½ cup fondant-frosting mix
   or confectioner's sugar
32 edible silver dragees
Pink and yellow mini-
   marshmallows

40 minutes preparation
20 minutes baking
Makes 16 small cakes

1 Preheat the oven to 350°F. Line two muffin tins with muffin liners.

2 Place the margarine, eggs, sugar, flour, and extract in a bowl and beat together for about 2 minutes until smooth. Half-fill each muffin liner with the mixture.

3 Bake for about 20 minutes, then cool the cakes on a wire cake rack. Cut the tops of the cakes level if they have peaked.

4 For the decoration, mix the confectioner's sugar with a little water to make a thin frosting. Add a little food coloring to the frosting to make an even color. Spoon a little on to each cake and spread out with a teaspoon.

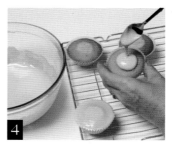

5 Cut a marshmallow in half and position as ears. Place a marshmallow in the center to form the snout. Position the dragees as eyes and cut a yellow marshmallow in half for the mouth.

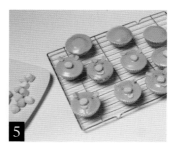

Blackberry Oysters

Freezer Friendly

I make a batch of these little pastries and freeze them. They are handy if you want to serve just a few with a selection of sandwiches.

Ingredients:

¾ cup pie pastry or pâte brisée
¼ cup butter or hard margarine
¼ cup superfine sugar
1¾ tbsp self-rising flour
¼ cup ground almonds
1 egg, beaten
A few drops of almond extract

Filling:

5 tbsp blackberry jam
¼ cup unsalted butter
½ cup confectioner's sugar

30 minutes preparation
20 minutes baking
Makes 16

1 Preheat the oven to 375°F. Grease two muffin tins. Roll out the pastry thinly, then cut out 16 3 inch rounds and press into the tins to line.

2 Beat the fat and sugar together until fluffy, then beat in the flour, almonds, egg, and extract. Place a heaped teaspoonful in each muffin cup and bake for about 20 minutes, until risen and golden. Cool on a wire cake rack.

3 When cold, scoop around the sponge filling with a knife and then place 1 teaspoon of jam in the base of each pastry shell.

4 For the filling, beat the butter with the confectioner's sugar until light and fluffy. Pipe or spoon a little buttercream on top of the jam, then replace the sponge filling and dust with confectioner's sugar to serve.

Cook's Tip:

To freeze, complete the cakes, but do not dust with confectioner's sugar. Freeze in a rigid plastic container for up to 2 months. Dust with confectioner's sugar before serving.

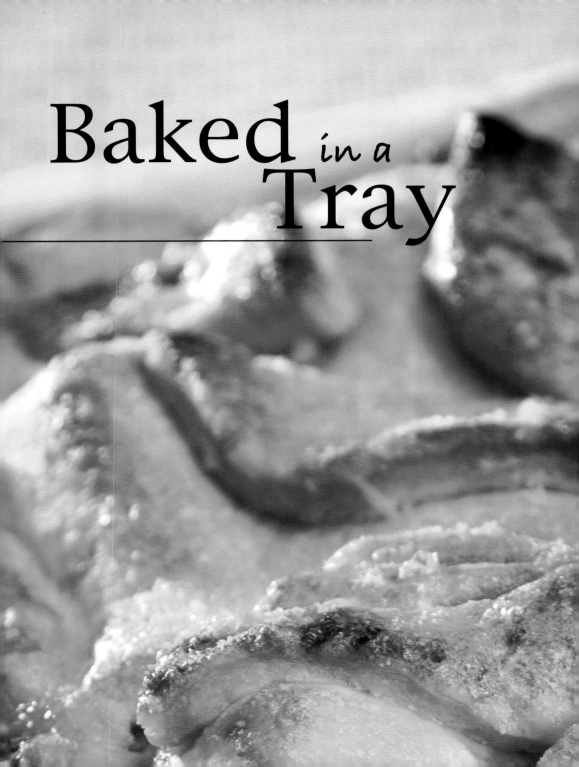

Baked *in a* Tray

Oaty Squares

Quick and Easy

Everybody loves these sweet, sticky, oaty squares (called flapjacks in England). I like to make mine with honey and add dried cranberries for their hint of sharpness, but try your own versions. Try adding dried fruits or apricots, cherries, nuts, or apple slices.

Ingredients:

- **½ cup butter or margarine**
- **⅓ cup maple syrup or honey**
- **⅓ cup soft, light-brown sugar**
- **¾ cup quick oats**
- **1¾ tbsp whole-wheat flour**
- **¼ cup dried cranberries or golden raisins**

10 minutes preparation

25 minutes baking

Makes 12

1 Preheat the oven to 350°F. Grease and line the base of an 8 inch shallow, square baking pan.

2 Put the butter, syrup or honey, and sugar in a saucepan and heat gently until dissolved.

3 Add the oats, flour, and cranberries or golden raisins and stir well. Spoon into the pan and spread level.

4 Bake for about 25 minutes, until golden. Mark into 12 fingers while still warm, then leave to cool in the pan. Peel the paper away and store in an airtight container until needed.

Cook's Tip:

To freeze, wrap a cold, oaty square tightly in aluminum foil. Keep frozen for up to 2 months.

Spicy Fudge Bake

spicy

If you are asked to bake for your child's school or a charity event, this frosted bake is an easy one to make from pantry ingredients.

Ingredients:

½ cup soft margarine
½ cup golden superfine
   sugar
⅓ cup whole-wheat flour
¼ cup self-rising flour
1 tsp baking powder
½ tsp ground cinnamon
2 eggs
2 tbsp milk
1 tbsp maple syrup

Frosting:

¾ cup golden
   confectioner's sugar
¼ cup softened butter
1 tbsp milk

20 minutes preparation
20 minutes baking
Makes 16 slices

1 Preheat the oven to 350°F. Grease and line a 7 x 11 inch shallow pan with nonstick parchment paper.

2 Place the margarine and sugar in a bowl and sift in the flours, baking powder, and spice. Add the eggs, milk, and syrup and beat for 2 minutes until smooth.

3 Spoon into the pan and smooth the top level. Bake for 20–25 minutes until the cake is springy and has shrunk away from the sides of the pan.

Loosen around the sides of the pan with a palette knife, then turn out to cool completely on a wire cake rack.

4 For the frosting, place the frosting ingredients in a bowl and beat until smooth. Swirl the frosting over the top of the cake with a palette knife.

5 Place the cake on a board and then cut the cake into 16 oblong slices with a sharp knife.

Espresso Squares

Freezer Friendly

If you like coffee, you'll love these moist little squares with a coffee-cream lattice. I often make a batch of these, serving half and storing the other half in the freezer.

Ingredients:

3/4 cup self-rising flour
1 tsp baking powder
3/4 cup soft margarine
3/4 cup soft, light-brown sugar
3 eggs
2 tbsp coffee extract

Frosting:

1/3 cup softened butter
3/4 cup golden confectioner's sugar, sifted
1 tbsp coffee extract

30 minutes preparation
25 minutes baking
Makes 15 squares

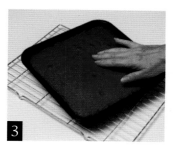

1 Preheat the oven to 350°F. Grease and line the base of a 9 inch square pan with nonstick parchment paper.

2 Sift the flour and baking powder into a bowl and add the remaining cake ingredients. Beat together with a wooden spoon for about 2 minutes until smooth.

3 Spoon into the pan and smooth the surface level. Bake for 25–30 minutes until well risen and firm. Test by pressing the center lightly with the fingertips. Cool in the pan for 5 minutes, then turn out on to a wire cake rack and peel away the lining paper.

4 To make the frosting, place the butter, sugar, and extract in a bowl and whisk until smooth. Spoon the icing into a pastry bag fitted with a star nozzle. Pipe a criss-cross lattice pattern over the top of the cake.

5 Place the cake on a board and cut into 15 squares, using a sharp knife.

Cook's Tip:

If you don't have a pastry bag, simply spread the frosting over with a palette knife, then make a wiggly pattern with a fork.

Millionaire's Shortbread

Something Special

You'll always be popular with your guests when you serve these chocolate-topped, luxury layers.

Ingredients:
- ½ cup butter, softened
- ¼ cup golden superfine sugar
- ¾ cup all-purpose flour

Topping:
- ¾ cup dark chocolate, broken into squares

Caramel:
- 14oz can evaporated milk
- 2 tbsp maple syrup
- ½ cup golden superfine sugar
- ½ cup butter

1 hour 30 minutes preparation
25 minutes baking
Makes 9 squares

1. Preheat the oven to 350°F. Grease and line the base of an 8 inch square pan with nonstick parchment paper.

2. Beat the butter and sugar together until pale and fluffy. Mix in the flour and knead in the bowl until smooth.

3. Press the mixture into the pan and prick the surface with a fork. Bake for 20–25 minutes until light golden. Cool in the pan on a wire cake rack.

4. To make the caramel layer, put the evaporated milk, syrup, sugar, and butter in a heavy-based saucepan. Heat gently until every grain of sugar has dissolved.

5. Bring to a boil and boil for 6–8 minutes, stirring continuously, until light golden and thickened. Pour the caramel over the shortbread base to cover it completely. Leave until cold and set.

6. Melt the chocolate in a bowl standing over a pan of warm water, or, alternately, in the microwave on low. Spread over the caramel with a palette knife and leave to cool and set. Mark into 9 squares to serve.

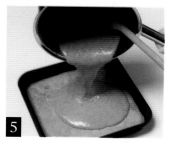

Bread & Butter Pudding

Family Favorite

Family desserts need not be expensive affairs. This favourite recipe in England uses up ordinary, sliced, white bread, making it into a creamy, light-as-air dessert.

Ingredients:

12 thin slices of white bread
$^1/_3$ cup butter, softened
$^1/_2$ cup golden raisins
Finely grated rind of 2 lemons
$^1/_2$ cup light-brown sugar
1$^1/_4$ cup milk
$^2/_3$ cup light cream
3 eggs
Few drops of vanilla extract

45 minutes preparation
40 minutes baking
Serves 6

1 Cut the crusts from the bread and spread one side of each slice with butter. Cut each slice in half diagonally, then in half again to make 4 triangles.

2 Butter a 6-cup-capacity, ovenproof pan or dish and arrange the triangles in an overlapping pattern, scattering the golden raisins, lemon rind, and sugar between the layers.

3 Beat the milk, cream, eggs, and extract together, pour over the bread, and leave to soak for 30 minutes.

4 Preheat the oven to 350°F. Bake the pudding for about 40 minutes, or until the slices are crisp and golden and the custard-sauce mixture has set.

5 Serve cut into squares, sprinkled with extra sugar, with heavy cream, or with dairy custard.

Cook's Tip:

For a variation, spread 3 tablespoons of orange marmalade on to the bread with the butter, and scatter over dried apricots instead of golden raisins.

Fall Crumble Bake

Family Favorite

Young or old, all the family love a fruit-based crumble. It must be the easiest dessert to make. If you make the crumble topping in the food processor, you won't even get your hands dirty.

Ingredients:

2 cups cooking apples, peeled, cored, and chopped
2 cups ripe plums, pitted, quartered
3 tbsp golden granulated sugar

Topping:

³/₄ cup all-purpose flour
¹/₃ cup butter or hard margarine, diced
¹/₄ cup golden superfine sugar

15 minutes preparation
40 minutes baking
Serves 6

1 Preheat the oven to 400°F. Put the apples in a heavy-based pan, add 1¹/₂ hot water and bring to a boil. Cover and simmer for 5 minutes.

2 Drain the apples and add the plums and sugar. Mix and place in an oblong shallow 6-cup-capacity dish or a 9 inch square, shallow baking pan.

3 To make the crumble topping, sift the flour into a

bowl and add the fat. Rub into the mixture with your fingertips until the mixture resembles fine crumbs, then stir in the sugar.

4 Spoon the mixture over the fruit in the dish and spread level. Bake for 35–40 minutes, or until the crumble topping is golden and the fruit is tender.

Cook's Tip:

If plums are not in season, use 2 cups firm, sweet pears. For a summer version, use 1 cup strawberries and 4 firm, sliced peaches mixed with 4 tablespoons of granulated sugar.

Lemon Meringue Squares

Easy Entertaining

These squares are a cross between a lemon meringue pie and a cake, so you can serve them either as a dessert or for afternoon tea.

Cake Layer:

¹/₃ cup butter
¹/₃ cup superfine sugar
2 eggs
¹/₂ cup self-rising flour

Meringue:

2 egg whites
¹/₂ cup superfine sugar

Lemon Filling:

¹/₄ cup butter
¹/₄ cup superfine sugar
2 egg yolks
Finely grated rind of 1 lemon
2 tbsp lemon juice

50 minutes preparation
1 hour baking
Makes 12

1 Preheat the oven to 325°F. Grease and line the base of a 7 x 11 inch baking pan with nonstick parchment paper.

2 Place the lemon-filling ingredients in a heatproof bowl over a pan of hot water and stir until the butter dissolves. The mixture should be thick enough to coat the back of a wooden spoon. Cool the mixture.

3 Make the cake layer. Beat the butter with the sugar until light and fluffy, then beat in the eggs, one at a time, adding a little flour with each. Fold in the remaining flour and spread into the pan.

4 Spread the cooled lemon filling over the top of the sponge mixture. Make the meringue topping. Whisk the egg whites until stiff, then fold in half the sugar and whisk again until stiff. Fold in the remaining sugar.

5 Spoon the meringue over the top of the filling, covering it completely. Bake for 1 hour until the top is crisp and light golden. Then, using a very sharp knife, cut into 12 squares.

Apple Pie for a Crowd

Easy Entertaining

I love making the most of the local varieties of apples available every fall, and really enjoy a trip to our local farmer's market to buy boxes of glorious fruits to bake into pies.

Pastry:

½ cup self-rising flour
1 cup all-purpose flour
¼ tsp salt
1 tbsp superfine sugar
¾ cup butter or hard
  margarine

Filling:

2lb cooking apples

Juice and finely grated rind
  of ½ lemon
2 tsp all-purpose flour
½ tsp ground cinnamon
½ tsp ground nutmeg
½ cup golden superfine
  sugar
1 tbsp butter
1 egg white, beaten
Confectioner's sugar to glaze

35 minutes preparation
45 minutes baking
Serves 6–8

1 To make the pastry, sift the flours, salt, and sugar into a bowl. Add the butter, cutting it into small cubes. Rub the fat into the flour with your fingertips until it resembles fine crumbs. Add 5–6 tablespoons of cold water and mix together with a knife. Knead to a soft dough, then wrap in plastic wrap and chill for 1 hour.

2 Preheat the oven to 400°F. Mix the flour, spices, and sugar. Peel, core, and chop the apples, then toss in the lemon juice, rind, and sugar mixture. Place in the base of a 6-cup-capacity oblong pan or dish, or a 9 inch round pie dish, and dot with butter.

3 Roll two-thirds of the pastry out to an oblong 1 inch larger than the top of the dish. Moisten the edges of the dish with water. Roll thin strips to make a border around the pie dish and then press into the sides.

4 Place the pastry lid on top, cutting a hole in the center. Roll out the trimmings and make into fancy shapes to decorate. Brush with beaten egg white and sprinkle lightly with sugar. Bake for 40–45 minutes until crisp and golden.

Cherry Cheesecake Slices

These cherry cheesecake slices make the ideal dessert for a picnic, or make a pan of them ahead of time and serve them after a barbecue.

Ingredients:

6oz whole-wheat cookies
1/3 cup butter, melted
1³/₄ tbsp golden granulated sugar

Topping:

14oz jar pitted morello cherries
2 tsp arrowroot

Filling:

1¹/₂ cups whole-fat cream cheese
¹/₂ cup natural superfine sugar
2 eggs, beaten
¹/₂ tsp vanilla extract
2 tsp lemon juice

45 minutes preparation
30 minutes baking
Makes 12 slices

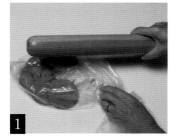

1 Preheat the oven to 350°F. Grease and line the base of a 7 x 11 inch oblong pan with nonstick parchment paper. Place the cookies in a strong plastic Baggie and crush into crumbs by tapping with a rolling pin.

2 Melt the butter in a heavy-based pan and mix in the cookie crumbs and sugar. Stir together, then spoon into the pan and spread over the base evenly.

3 Soften the cream cheese together with the sugar, then beat in the eggs, extract, and lemon juice until smooth. Pour over the cookie base in the pan. Bake for about 30 minutes until the filling is risen, firm, and golden. Cool in the pan, then chill. When cold, remove from the pan and peel away the paper.

4 To make the cherry topping, dissolve the arrowroot powder with 2 tablespoons of juice from the cherries. Place the cherries and remaining juice in a heavy-based pan and heat until the juices thicken. Then spoon the cherry mixture over the baked base.

5 Leave to cool and set, then cut into 12 slices with a sharp knife.

Deluxe Bread Pudding

Freezer Friendly

This easy recipe will get you out of a fix when you have promised to contribute to the kids' bake sale—and have then forgotten to buy any ingredients! Use up all the leftover bread in the house and add a few ingredients from the pantry.

Ingredients:

1lb stale bread, crusts removed
Finely grated rind and juice of 1 orange
1¼ cup milk
1 egg
1 cup dried mixed fruit
½ cup soft, dark-brown sugar
⅓ cup soft margarine
1 tsp mixed spice
3 tbsp fine-cut orange marmalade, warmed
1 tbsp ginger wine or orange liqueur (optional)
2 tbsp golden granulated sugar

30 minutes preparation
1 hour baking
Makes 16 slices

1 Preheat the oven to 375°F. Grease a 7 x 11 inch oblong pan.

2 Cut the bread into small pieces. Place in a large bowl with the orange rind, juice, and milk. Leave to soak for 15 minutes. Mash with a fork to break up the pieces.

3 Add the egg, dried fruit, brown sugar, margarine, spice, marmalade, and liqueur and stir together.

4 Spread into the pan and smooth the surface level. Bake for about 1 hour, or until firm. Cool in the pan and then dredge the top with granulated sugar.

5 Cut into 16 slices, then serve warm or cold.

Cook's Tip:

To freeze, wrap in aluminum foil. Freeze for up to 6 months.

Cookies

Melting Moments

Quick and Easy

These little cookies couldn't be easier to make. Just roll the mixture into a ball and pop in a piece of cherry. They really do melt in the mouth!

10 minutes preparation
15 minutes baking
Makes 16

Ingredients:

2³/₄ tbsp superfine sugar
¹/₄ cup butter or hard margarine
A few drops of vanilla extract
³/₄ cup self-rising flour
1 tbsp rolled oats or shredded coconut
4 candied cherries

1 Preheat the oven to 350°F. Grease two cookie sheets.

2 Beat the sugar, butter or margarine, and vanilla extract together until fluffy.

3 Sift in the flour and mix with your fingertips to make a soft dough. Divide into 16 pieces.

4 Roll each piece into a ball. Spread the oats or coconut out on to a plate and roll each ball to coat it. Flatten each ball slightly.

5 Cut each cherry into 4 and place 1 piece on every cookie. Place on the prepared cookie sheets and bake for about 15 minutes until the cookies are puffed up and pale golden in color.

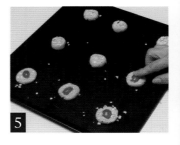

Cook's Tip:

Store the baked cookies in an airtight container, and they will keep crisp for up to 3 days. Do not store in a plastic food container as these are designed to keep in moisture and will make the cookies go soft.

𝒳

Coconut & Lemon Cookies

Freezer Friendly

Although these cookies may look plain, the combination of sharp lemon and sweet, crunchy coconut is extremely tasty.

Ingredients:

½ cup **butter or margarine**
½ cup **soft, light-brown sugar**
½ cup **all-purpose flour**
¼ cup **self-rising flour**
⅓ cup **quick oats**
¼ cup **shredded coconut**
1 **lemon**
1 tsp **vanilla extract**
1 **egg**

10 minutes preparation
12 minutes baking
Makes 24

1 Preheat the oven to 350°F. Grease two cookie sheets. Chop the butter or margarine into small cubes.

2 Stir the sugar, flours, oats, and coconut together in a bowl. Finely grate the zest from the lemon and add to the bowl.

3 Beat the egg and vanilla extract together and add to the bowl with 1 tablespoon of lemon juice. Then mix into a soft mixture.

4 Place 24 heaped teaspoons of mixture on to the cookie sheets and flatten out slightly. Bake for 12 minutes until light golden and firm. Remove from the cookie sheets with a palette knife and cool on wire cake racks.

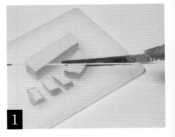

Cook's Tip:

Space the cookies evenly on the cookie sheets, leaving room for them to spread. Flatten them with wetted fingers into neat shapes.

Crunchy Peanut-butter Cookies

Quick and Easy

Who can resist these crunchy morsels? You can make these cookies from pantry ingredients—a great way to keep the kids busy on a rainy day.

Ingredients:

- ¼ **cup soft margarine**
- ½ **cup crunchy peanut butter**
- ⅓ **cup superfine sugar**
- ½ **cup self-rising flour**
- ½ **tsp baking soda**
- 1 **egg, beaten**
- ¼ **cup quick oats**
- ¼ **cup shelled peanuts, chopped**
- 1–2 **tbsp milk**

10 minutes preparation
10–12 minutes baking
Makes 16

1 Preheat the oven to 375°F. Grease two cookie sheets.

2 Beat the margarine, peanut butter, and sugar together until light and fluffy.

3 Now sift in the flour and baking soda and stir together with the egg, oats, peanuts, and enough milk to form a soft dough.

4 Roll heaped tablespoons of the mixture into balls. Space them well apart on the cookie sheets, slightly flatten, then press down with a fork.

5 Bake for 15 minutes until golden. Cool on the cookie sheets for 2 minutes to firm up, then, with a palette knife, lift them on to a wire cake rack to cool.

Cook's Tip:

If you lightly wet your hands when you roll the dough into balls, you will find that the mixture does not stick.

Giant Choc-chip Cookies

Family Favorite

You'll find these giant cookies on sale in fancy bakers'—delicious, but they can be expensive! Make this version for far fewer cents.

Ingredients:

³/₄ cup self-rising flour
1³/₄ tbsp cocoa powder
¹/₃ cup soft, slightly salted butter or margarine
¹/₄ cup granulated sugar
¹/₄ cup golden superfine sugar
1 egg, beaten
1 tsp vanilla extract
¹/₄ cup dark chocolate chips
1³/₄ tbsp white chocolate chips
2 tsp milk

15 minutes preparation
15 minutes baking
Makes 12–14

1 Preheat the oven to 350°F. Lightly grease two cookie sheets. Sift the flour and cocoa into a bowl.

2 Place all the ingredients (except for the chocolate chips) in a bowl and mix thoroughly to make a soft, smooth dough. Gradually work in the chocolate chips.

3 Place 6 large spoonfuls of the mixture, spaced well apart, on each cookie sheet and flatten slightly with the back of a wetted spoon.

4 Bake for 15–20 minutes until risen, light golden, and just firm to the touch. Leave on the cookie sheets to firm for 2–3 minutes, then lift on to a wire cake rack to cool using a palette knife.

Cook's Tip:

Don't be tempted to overcrowd the cookie sheets as the cookies will spread out during cooking. If you don't have enough cookie sheets, divide the mixture in half and reuse the same cookie sheet, cooling it and regreasing it each time.

Gingerbread Bears

Party Special

These cute little critters appeal to children of all ages. Make them for a children's party and just watch the adults sneak them off the plates!

Ingredients:

1 cup all-purpose flour
1 tsp baking soda
½ tsp ground ginger
½ tsp mixed spice
¼ cup butter or hard
**   margarine**
¼ cup maple syrup
¼ cup soft, dark-brown sugar
½ egg, beaten

To Decorate:

¼ cup confectioner's
**   sugar for royal icing**

30 minutes preparation
10 minutes baking
Makes 20 large or 28 small cookies

1 Preheat the oven to 350°F and grease two cookie sheets. Sift the flour into a bowl with the baking soda and spices. Melt the butter in a saucepan with the maple syrup and sugar.

2 Pour the melted mixture into the dry ingredients, add the egg, and mix to a soft dough. Knead gently. The dough will be sticky at first, but it will firm as it cools.

3 Roll out to about ⅛ inch thickness and cut out fancy shapes. Bake for about 10–12 minutes and leave to firm for 2 minutes. Then remove to wire cake racks with a palette knife.

4 To decorate, mix the confectioner's sugar with water to make a piping consistency. Place in a small pastry bag and pipe on buttons, bow ties, frills, or fancy decorations.

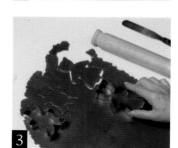

Cook's Tip:

Keep checking the cookies toward the end of the baking time as they can overbrown very quickly.

Cantucci Biscotti

No Fat

These delicious almond cookies are baked until they are very dry. They are meant to be served dipped into a sweet Italian wine called *vin santo*, but are equally delicious with creamy desserts or coffee.

Ingredients:

1 cup all-purpose flour
2 tsp baking powder
1/4 tsp salt
3/4 cup superfine sugar
2 eggs
1 tsp vanilla extract
1 tbsp amaretto liqueur
1/2 cup blanched whole almonds

45 minutes preparation
35 minutes baking
Makes 24

1 Preheat the oven to 350°F. Grease and flour two cookie sheets.

2 Sift the flour, baking powder, and salt into a bowl and stir in the sugar. Beat the eggs with the extract and liqueur. Add to the bowl with the almonds and mix to a very soft dough.

3 Divide into 4 equal pieces and roll each into a log shape about 6 inches long. Chill in the freezer for 5 minutes to firm the dough.

Place on the cookie sheets and bake for 20 minutes, or until the cookies are golden.

4 Remove from the oven and cut each log into 1/2 inch slices while still warm. Separate them and lay on a cookie sheet.

5 Return the cookies to the oven and bake for 15 minutes until golden, turning them over halfway through the cooking. Cool completely, then store in an airtight container.

Cook's Tip:

Place two pieces of dough only on each cookie sheet as the dough will spread out during baking.

Butterscotch Nut Thins

Easy Entertaining

These luxurious, wafer-thin cookies are delicious served with vanilla ice cream or on their own with a cup of coffee. They could not be easier to make. Just melt the mixture together in a saucepan.

Ingredients:

Sheets of rice paper
2³/₄ tsp butter
2³/₄ tsp superfine sugar
2 tsp heavy cream or rich whole milk
¹/₃ cup chopped or sliced almonds

10 minutes preparation
8 minutes baking
Makes 14–16

1 Preheat the oven to 350°F. Line two cookie sheets with sheets of rice paper, overlapping them if necessary.

2 Place the butter, sugar, and cream in a heavy-based pan and heat gently until melted. Bring to a boil, then simmer for 30 seconds until light and foaming. Remove from the heat, stir in the nuts, and mix thoroughly.

3 Place 8 heaped teaspoonfuls on the rice paper on each sheet. Space well apart as the cookies will spread out during cooking.

4 Bake for 8 minutes until the cookies are a medium-golden color. Leave on the cookie sheets until firm, then lift up and break off the extra rice paper. Store the cookies in an airtight container.

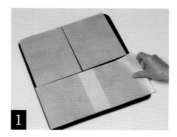

Cook's Tip:

These cookies will turn brown and caramelize very quickly, so be careful to watch them toward the end of cooking.

Fruity Florentines

Easy Entertaining

You'll find these luxury cookies on sale in expensive delis and food departments. Make your own, colorful versions, full of good things, as an ideal gift for a hostess, or even a super Christmas gift.

Ingredients:

⅓ cup butter
½ cup confectioner's sugar, sifted
4 tbsp heavy cream
1 tbsp candied cherries, chopped
1 tbsp angelica, chopped
1 tbsp crystallized ginger, chopped
2¾ tbsp all-purpose flour

2 tsp lemon juice
⅓ cup mixed peel
1¾ tbsp currants
⅓ cup sliced almonds

Topping:

⅓ cup dark chocolate, melted

25 minutes preparation
10–12 minutes baking
Makes 15–20

1. Preheat the oven to 375°F. Line two cookie sheets with nonstick parchment paper. Gently heat the butter, confectioner's sugar, and cream in a saucepan.

2. When the butter has melted, add the rest of the ingredients and mix together in the pan with a wooden spoon.

3. Spoon dessertspoonfuls of the mixture on to the cookie sheets, leaving a 3 inch space between each one to allow the mixture to spread. Bake for 10–12 minutes until the edges are golden and lacy. Cool the cookie sheets for 10 minutes, then transfer to a wire cake rack.

4. When cold, brush the backs of the cookies with melted chocolate and leave to set for 30 minutes.

Cook's Tip:

If the cookies spread unevenly, pat them into a round shape, using a knife or cookie cutter, while still hot on the sheets.

Shortbread

Easy Entertaining

I make this crumbly, buttery favorite every December for New Year's Eve. We always observe the Scots tradition of first-footing—taking some shortbread and a piece of coal to our friends and neighbors.

Ingredients:

¹/₂ cup butter
¹/₄ cup superfine sugar
Finely grated zest of ¹/₂ lemon
¹/₂ cup all-purpose flour
1³/₄ tbsp rice starch or cornstarch
Superfine sugar for dusting

30 minutes preparation
25 minutes baking
Makes 8 wedges

1 Preheat the oven to 325°F. Grease a cookie sheet. Beat the butter and sugar together with the lemon zest until pale and fluffy.

2 Sift the flour and rice starch or cornstarch into the mixture and bring it together with your fingertips to make a soft dough. Roll out the dough on a floured surface to make a 7 inch circle.

3 Place on the cookie sheet and crimp the edges with your fingers.

4 Mark into 8 wedges, then prick the dough all over with a fork. Chill in the freezer for 5 minutes.

5 Bake for 25–30 minutes until the shortbread is pale golden and firm to the touch. Cool on the cookie sheet for 15 minutes, then transfer to a wire cake rack until cold. Cut into wedges and serve sprinkled with superfine sugar.

Cook's Tip:

Store the shortbread in an airtight container for up to 1 week or freeze, wrapped in aluminum foil, for up to 2 months.

Mocha Pinwheels

Freezer Friendly

Keep this fancy cookie dough stored in the freezer until you are ready to bake it, then you'll always have fresh cookies to offer around.

1 hour preparation
20 minutes baking
Makes 18

Vanilla Layer:

1/4 cup butter or hard
    margarine, softened
1³/4 tbsp superfine sugar
1/3 cup all-purpose flour
A few drops of vanilla
    extract

Mocha Layer:

1/4 cup butter or hard
    margarine, softened
1³/4 tbsp superfine sugar
1/3 cup all-purpose flour
1 tbsp cocoa powder
1 tsp coffee extract

1 Place the ingredients for the two doughs into separate bowls. Bring the ingredients for the vanilla dough together and bind to a soft dough with 1 tablespoon of water. Wrap and freeze for 15 minutes.

2 Bring the mocha ingredients together and bind to a soft dough. Wrap and freeze for 15 minutes.

3 Roll out each dough to a rectangle measuring 7 x 10 inches. Brush the mocha dough with a little water, then place the vanilla dough on top.

4 Roll both doughs together like a jelly roll from the narrow end. Wrap the dough and chill for 30 minutes, or freeze until firm.

5 Preheat the oven to 350°F. Grease two cookie sheets. Cut the dough into 18 slices, each 1/4 inch wide.

6 Place on the cookie sheets and space well apart. Bake for 15–20 minutes until firm and pale golden. Cool on the cookie sheets for 2 minutes to firm, then transfer to a wire cake rack.

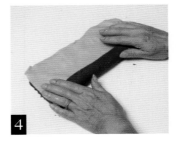

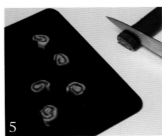

Something
Special

Piña Colada Gateau

Party Special

This cake makes an ideal centerpiece for a summer party in the garden, or a special birthday cake. Make it ahead of time and store in the fridge for up to 1 day.

Ingredients:

3/4 cup soft margarine
3/4 cup superfine sugar
3 eggs, beaten
3/4 cup self-rising flour
1/4 cup shredded coconut

Filling and Decoration:

2 cups heavy cream
1 tablespoon Malibu or
    coconut liqueur
4 slices canned pineapple
    rings
1/4 cup coconut curls

45 minutes preparation
25 minutes baking
Serves 10

1 Preheat the oven to 350°F. Grease and line two 8 inch round pans.

2 Make the cake bases. Place all the cake ingredients in a large bowl and beat together for about 2 minutes until smooth.

3 If the mixture is too dry, add 2 tablespoons of milk to form a soft consistency that drops from a spoon. Spoon the mixture into the pans and smooth level.

4 Bake for 25 minutes until the cakes are firm and shrink away from the pans. Stand for 5 minutes, then cool on a wire cake rack. Spread the coconut curls on to a cookie sheet and toast lightly for 1–2 minutes.

5 To make the filling, whip the cream until it forms soft peaks, then fold in the liqueur. Chop 3 of the pineapple rings and fold into half the cream and use to sandwich the cakes together.

6 Cut the remaining pineapple ring into 8 wedges. Spread cream around the sides of the cake and roll in the coconut curls. Spread cream over the top of the cake. Put the remaining cream in a pastry bag with a star nozzle. Pipe 8 rosettes or stars around the edge and decorate each with a pineapple wedge.

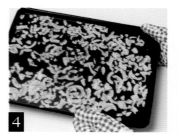

Apricot Meringue Mountain

Easy Entertaining

This is one of my favorite desserts: light-as-a-feather meringue, sandwiched together with luscious cream and fruit. Try it with a fresh strawberry filling instead of apricot.

Ingredients:

1 cup superfine sugar
4 large egg whites
$1/4$ tsp cream of tartar

Filling:

$1^1/4$ cups heavy cream
14oz can apricots in syrup

20 minutes preparation
50 minutes baking
Serves 6

1 Preheat the oven to 300°F. Draw a 9 inch circle on a sheet of nonstick parchment paper and a 6 inch circle on another and place the papers on two cookie sheets.

2 Place the egg whites in a large, clean, and dry bowl and whisk with the cream of tartar until stiff.

3 Gradually add the sugar, 1 tablespoon at a time, until the meringue has become stiff and glossy.

4 Spoon the mixture on to the papers and spread out to fill the circles. Build or flick up the sides to form a rim. Turn the oven down to 275°F and bake for 50 minutes, or until the meringue is crisp. Cool completely on wire cake racks.

5 For the filling, whip the cream until stiff and spread in the large meringue shell. Drain the apricots and place on top of the cream. Top with the small meringue and serve immediately.

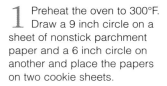

Cook's Tip:

- To make sure that the bowl is completely grease-free, scald it out with boiling water and dry with paper towels. If there is any grease at all in the bowl, the egg whites will not whisk up.
- To test if the meringue is crisp and dry, push it slightly on the cookie sheet. If it slides away from the paper easily, it is ready.

Christmas Log

Party Special

The yule log, served the day after Christmas, is a traditional part of my Christmas time.

Ingredients:

2 tbsp cocoa
3 eggs
¹/2 cup superfine sugar
¹/2 cup all-purpose flour
2 tbsp superfine sugar

Decoration:

1 tbsp cocoa powder
1 cup unsalted butter
2 cups golden
   confectioner's sugar
3 tbsp milk
Confectioner's sugar

45 minutes preparation

15 minutes baking

Serves 6

1 Preheat the oven to 400°F. Grease and line a 12 x 8 inch jelly-roll pan with nonstick parchment paper.

2 Blend the cocoa powder with 3 tablespoons of boiling water and mix until smooth. Whisk the eggs and sugar in a heatproof bowl, set over a pan of hot water for 8 minutes until very pale and thick, or until the whisks leave a trail on the surface when lifted. Remove from the heat.

3 Sift in half the flour and fold in gently. Fold in the remaining flour with the cocoa mixture and stir until evenly blended. Pour the mixture into the pan and bake for 10–15 minutes until springy. Sprinkle the superfine sugar over a sheet of nonstick paper.

4 Turn the sponge on to the paper, peel away the lining paper, and trim the sponge edges. Roll up from the long side, with the paper inside, and cool. When cold, carefully unroll the cake.

5 Make the frosting. Blend the cocoa to a paste with 2 tablespoons of boiling water. Beat the confectioner's sugar with the butter and milk until fluffy. Spread one-quarter of the buttercream over the jelly roll and roll up. Add the cocoa mixture to the remaining buttercream and beat until smooth. Spread over the top and sides of the jelly roll with a palette knife. Dust with confectioner's sugar just before serving.

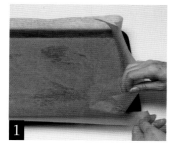

Cook's Tip:

To ensure that the cake rises evenly, tilt the jelly-roll pan so that the mixture covers the surface and fills the corners evenly.

Birthday Cake

Party Special

If you are asked to make a birthday cake in a hurry, this quick and easy one fits the bill. There is no difficult frosting, and you can vary the colors and decorations to suit all ages.

Ingredients:

³/₄ cup soft margarine
³/₄ cup superfine sugar
3 eggs, beaten
³/₄ cup self-rising flour
¹/₂ tsp baking powder
1 tsp vanilla extract
2 tbsp milk
Pink food coloring

Filling and Frosting:

¹/₂ cup apricot jam, sieved, warmed
1¹/₄ cup ready-to-use rolled fondant
Colored birthday candles and ribbons to decorate

35 minutes preparation
25 minutes baking
Serves 8

1 Preheat the oven to 375°F. Grease 2 x 7¹/₂ inch round pans and line the bases with nonstick parchment paper. Put all the cake ingredients (except the coloring) in a bowl.

2 Beat for 2 minutes until pale and fluffy. Divide the mixture in two and color one half pink. Spoon into the pans and spread the tops level. Bake for 20–25 minutes, or until just firm to the touch. Turn the cake out to cool on a wire cake rack.

3 Spread one cake with a third of the jam, then top with the second cake. Spread the remaining jam over the top and sides.

4 Color the fondant pale pink, then roll out on a surface dusted with confectioner's sugar to a circle large enough to cover the top and sides of the cake. Lift on to the cake with both hands and smooth into position. Trim away the edges and press the candles into the top. Tie ribbons around the sides.

Cook's Tip:

Use paste food coloring to color ready-to-use fondant as liquid food coloring will make the fondant wet and unmanageable.

Rich Fruitcake

Easy Entertaining

I always make this rich fruitcake 3–4 months ahead for Christmas or a special anniversary. This allows time for the flavors to mellow and the texture to become moist.

Ingredients:

4 cups mixed, dried fruit
1/4 cup candied cherries, washed, chopped
3 tbsp dark rum
Finely grated rind and juice of 1 lemon
1 cup soft, dark-brown sugar
1 cup butter, softened
2 tbsp molasses
5 eggs, beaten
1 cup all-purpose flour
1 tbsp mixed spice

1 hour preparation
3 1/2 hours baking
Serves 10–12

1 Place the fruit in a large saucepan with 2 tablespoons of the rum and the lemon juice and rind, and heat to a simmer. Heat for 5 minutes, turning the fruit over in the liquid with a wooden spoon. Pour the fruit into a bowl, cover, and leave to stand for 24 hours.

2 Preheat the oven to 300°F. Grease and double-line the base and sides of an 8 inch round, deep pan. Beat the butter and sugar until fluffy.

3 Beat in the eggs gradually, adding 1 teaspoon of flour with each addition. Beat in the molasses, then sift in the flour and the spice.

4 Add the soaked fruit and stir well until the mixture is smooth. Spoon into the pan and smooth the top evenly.

5 Bake for 1 hour, then reduce the temperature to 275°F and bake for a further 3–3 1/2 hours, or until a skewer inserted into the middle comes out cleanly.

6 Spoon the remaining tablespoon of rum over the warm cake and leave to cool in the pan. When cold, wrap in parchment paper, then tightly wrap in aluminum foil and store for 1–3 months.

Christmas Cake

Something Special

Follow these easy steps to decorate the ideal Christmas cake. Add a different ribbon to make an anniversary or christening cake.

Ingredients:

1 x 8 inch rich fruitcake (see page 241)
10 inch cardboard cake round
4 tbsp sieved apricot jam
3 cups almond paste
4$^{1}/_{2}$ cups ready-to-use rolled fondant
Golden dragees
Wired ribbon

1 hour 30 minutes preparation
3 days drying
Serves 10–12

1 Place the cake on the cake round and brush all over with sieved apricot jam. Roll out one-third of the almond paste on a surface dusted with confectioner's sugar. Using the pan as a guide, cut out a round, slightly larger than the top of the cake. Lift the disk of almond paste on to the cake with a rolling pin.

2 Use a length of string to measure the length and height of the sides of the cake. Roll the remaining almond paste to these measurements in a long strip. Roll up the strip, then loosely unroll around the cake, and press the top and sides of the paste together. Leave the almond paste to dry out for 3 days in a cool place.

3 On a surface dusted with confectioner's sugar, roll out the ready-to-use fondant to make a circle large enough to cover the top and sides of the cake. Brush the almond paste with a little water to dampen it. Lift the fondant over the cake to position it, then smooth down over the top and sides, and press on to the cake. Trim away the edges.

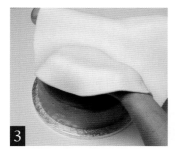

4 While the fondant is soft, mark lines across the top with the edge of a palette knife or a plastic rule. Mark another set in the opposite direction to make a square, quilted effect. Place a golden dragee in each square. Trim the cake with a festive ribbon to finish.

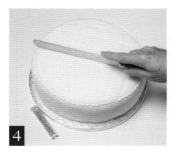

Gingerbread House

Party Special

This is a great way to keep the kids occupied in the days before Christmas.

Ingredients:

¹/₃ cup soft, dark-brown
  sugar
¹/₂ cup maple syrup
¹/₂ cup molasses
¹/₃ cup hard margarine
2 cups all-purpose flour
2 tsp ground ginger
2 egg yolks

1 tsp ground mixed spice
2 tsp baking soda

Decoration:

2 cups royal-icing mix
1 packet colored candies

1 hour preparation
10 minutes baking per sheet
Makes 1 house

1 Draw and cut out templates (see page 252) on paperboard as follows: 2 roof pieces, 6 x 8 inches; 2 sides, 2¹/₂ x 8 inches; 2 gables, 4 x 6¹/₂ inches, rising to a point; 1 chimney piece, 2 inches deep; 2 chimney sides, 2 inches deep, with a sloping side; 1 chimney piece, ³/₄ x 2 inches.

2 Preheat the oven to 375°F. Put the sugar, syrup, molasses, and margarine in a pan and heat gently until melted. Sift the flour, ginger, mixed spice, and baking soda into a bowl. Stir in the egg yolks and the melted mixture.

3 Knead to a soft dough. Halve the dough and keep half covered. While still warm, roll the dough out between two sheets of nonstick parchment paper. Lift the top paper away and cut around the paperboard template. Lift excess pastry from the paper. Place the gingerbreads on the paper on a cookie sheet and bake for 8–10 minutes. Leave flat to cool. Repeat with remaining trimmings and dough.

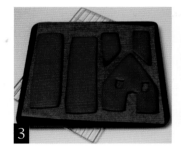

4 When all the pieces are cold and stiff, assemble the house. Make up the royal-icing mix and pipe along the wall edges. Join the walls together on a cake round, press, and leave to set. Fix on the roof pieces and then the chimney. Pipe on decorative frosting to resemble snow. Decorate the roof with candy.

Chocolate Mousse Cake

Quick and Easy

This party gateau looks complicated, but it is easy to make. Just swirl the two sets of whipped cream on top for a marbled effect.

Ingredients:

2 tbsp cocoa
³/₄ cup soft margarine
³/₄ cup golden superfine sugar
3 eggs
³/₄ cup self-rising flour
1 tsp baking powder
2 tbsp plain yogurt

Filling and Topping:

2 cups whipping cream
¹/₃ cup dark chocolate, melted

30 minutes preparation
25 minutes baking
Serves 8

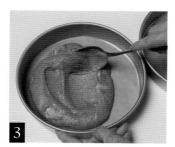

1 Preheat the oven to 350°F. Grease and line the bases of 2 x 7¹/₂ inch round pans with nonstick parchment paper.

2 In a large bowl, blend the cocoa with 3 tablespoons of boiling water, then cool. Add the remaining cake ingredients to the bowl and beat for 2 minutes until smooth.

3 Divide between the pans, smooth level, and bake for 20–25 minutes until springy. Cool on a wire cake rack.

4 For the filling and topping, whip the cream until firm,

then divide between two bowls. Add the melted chocolate to one bowl and stir until blended. Spread a little chocolate cream on to one sponge layer and use to sandwich the cakes.

5 Spoon alternate tablespoons of chocolate cream and plain cream on top of the cake. Roughly swirl with a palette knife to make a marbled pattern. Refrigerate until served.

Cook's Tip:

It is easy to melt the chocolate in a microwave. Break the chocolate into pieces, place in a microwave-proof bowl and use the "low" setting.

Black Forest Cake

Easy Entertaining

Ingredients:

5 eggs
³/₄ cup superfine sugar
¹/₃ cup unsalted butter, melted
¹/₄ cup all-purpose flour
¹/₄ cup cocoa powder

Filling and Decoration:

1 cup dark chocolate, melted
15oz can or jar of pitted black cherries, drained
4 tbsp kirsch
2 tbsp morello-cherry jam
2¹/₂ cups heavy cream

1 hour preparation
25 minutes baking
Serves 8

1 Preheat the oven to 350°F. Grease and line the bases of 2 x 8 inch round pans and dust lightly with flour.

2 Place the eggs and sugar in a large bowl set over a pan of hot water and whisk continuously until thick and pale, for about 5 minutes. Remove from the heat. Continue whisking for about 10 minutes until the mixture cools and falls in a thick ribbon.

3 Cool the melted butter. Sift the flour and cocoa into the mixture, then fold in gently. Pour the butter into the mixture in a slow stream and fold in.

4 Divide the mixture between the pans and bake for about 25 minutes until springy to the touch. Cool in the pans for 15 minutes, then turn out on to a wire cake rack.

When completely cold, cut each cake in half horizontally.

5 Spread the melted chocolate out on a clean surface in a thin layer. When just setting, pull a long, thin-bladed knife across the chocolate at an angle, and, in a sawing action, scrape the chocolate into thin curls. Repeat using all the chocolate.

6 Spread the cut sponges with cream and sandwich together. Place one on a serving dish, spread with jam. Scatter over half the cherries, top with cream, and place the remaining cake on top. Sprinkle the top cake with kirsch, then cover the whole cake with the remaining cream. Press the chocolate curls on to the sides. Decorate the top with cherries and chocolate.

White-chocolate Cake

Party Special

This delicate cake is smothered in a delightful white-chocolate cream. It is delicious served with fresh strawberries or raspberries in the summer.

Ingredients:

¹/₄ cup white chocolate
³/₄ cup butter or hard
**   margarine**
³/₄ cup superfine sugar
3 eggs, beaten
³/₄ cup self-rising flour
Finely grated zest of ¹/₂ a
**   lemon**

Filling and Topping:

²/₃ cup whipping cream
3 tbsp chocolate-nut spread
1 cup white chocolate
³/₄ cup sour cream

30 minutes preparation
20–25 minutes baking
Serves 8

1 Preheat the oven to 350°F. Grease and line the bases of 2 x 7¹/₂ inch round pans with nonstick parchment paper. Then grate the white chocolate finely.

2 Place the butter and sugar in a bowl and beat with an electric mixer until soft and fluffy. Gradually add the eggs, using a little flour with each addition. Fold in the flour, zest, and grated chocolate.

3 Spoon into the pans and spread level. Bake for 20–25 minutes until golden and just firm to the touch. Turn out to cool on a wire cake rack.

4 For the filling, whip the whipping cream until stiff, then divide in half. Mix half with the chocolate-nut spread and use to sandwich the cakes together.

5 For the topping, break the white chocolate into pieces and melt in the microwave on low. Alternately, melt in a bowl set over a pan of warm water. Beat together with the sour cream and then cool for 5 minutes. When cold, fold in the whipped cream and spread over the top and sides of the cake.

Gingerbread House

Template

Cut out: 2 gable ends (one with a door and windows)
           2 roof pieces
           2 sides
           1 set of chimney pieces

side

chimney pieces

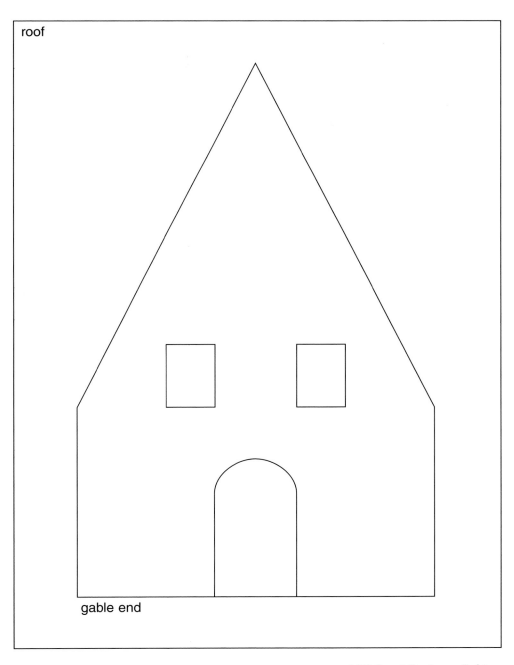

roof

gable end

Index

Credits & Acknowledgements

I would like to thank Progress Bakeware for supplying the Good Housekeeping range of bakeware and Mermaid Cookware for the utensils in the step-by-step photography. Also, thanks to Billington's Sugars for supplying their unrefined sugars for baking.

Thanks to Harrison Fisher and Co. (www.premiercutlery.co.uk) for supplying the knives and some of the small kitchen utensils also used in the step-by-step pictures.

Thanks also to Colin Bowling and Paul Forrester and the many cake tasters at Britannia Studios.

Kate's Book